COSMOPOIESIS

The Renaissance Experiment

Cosmopoiesis means 'world-making,' and in this erudite, polemical book, Professor Mazzotta traces how major medieval and Renaissance thinkers invented their worlds through utopias, magic, science, art, and theatre. The Renaissance is usually read from a Cartesian or Hegelian (via Burckhardt) perspective. It is viewed as a time of individualities or it is studied in terms of disembodied ideas and abstract forms. Mazzotta calls for a new approach: the necessity to study the Renaissance in terms of the ongoing conversation of the arts and sciences. His is an encyclopedic grasp that takes into consideration literature, philosophy, politics, history, and theology.

The book's theoretical premise lies in the thought of the eighteenth-century Italian philosopher Giambattista Vico. Vico's own reading of the Renaissance, available in his *New Science*, is obliquely, yet clearly, reposed as the alternative interpretive key for opening up the deeper imaginative concerns of this extraordinary period of Western history.

By a series of rigorous analyses of texts by such writers as Poliziano, Ariosto, Machiavelli, Bacon, Shakespeare, and Cervantes, *Cosmopoiesis* highlights the ongoing dialogue between literature and philosophy (or literature and science, or, in Vichian terms, philology and philosophy) in some of the central texts of the time.

In this dialogue across time and the barriers of space, the aesthetic world – 'the world of the pastoral, romances, epics, utopian fictions, the theatre, and the lyric' – far from signalling an evasion of history, is steadily and vitally engaged with the most pressing exigencies of the time. Consistently, the analyses conducted in *Cosmopoiesis* come to grips with these exigencies: the power of science, the relationship between politics and science, and the emergence of a new ethics in the midst of the secretive techniques by new elites in their exercise of political power. Above all, these central texts argue for a necessary reconstitution of the unity of knowledge, for the 'encyclopedic' compass of the arts and sciences.

(Goggio Publication Series, Toronto Italian Studies)

GIUSEPPE MAZZOTTA is Charles C. and Dorathea S. Dilley Professor of Italian Literature and Culture at Yale University.

TORONTO ITALIAN STUDIES

Goggio Publication Series
General Editor: Olga Zorzi Pugliese

GIUSEPPE MAZZOTTA

COSMOPOIESIS
The Renaissance Experiment

UNIVERSITY OF TORONTO PRESS
Toronto Buffalo London

© University of Toronto Press Incorporated 2001
Toronto Buffalo London

ISBN 0-8020-3551-5 (cloth)
ISBN 0-8020-8421-4 (paper)

Emilio Goggio Publication Series, Toronton Italian Studies
Editor: Olga Pugliese

National Library of Canada Cataloguing in Publication Data

Mazzotta, Giuseppe, 1942–
 Cosmopoiesis : the Renaissance experiment

 (Toronto Italian studies) (Emilio Goggio publication series)
 Lectures entitled Constructing worlds : Renaissance experiment, delivered
 at Victoria College on Oct. 7, 14, and 21, 1999, and one additional essay.

 Includes bibliographical references.
 ISBN 0-8020-3551-5 (bound)   ISBN 0-8020-8421-4 (pbk.)

 1. European literature – Renaissance, 1450–1600 – History and criticism.
 2. Italian literature – 16th century – History and criticism.   3. Philosophy,
 Renaissance.   I. Title.   II. Series.   III. Series: Goggio publications series.

 PN721.M39 2001   809'.894'09031   C2001-930246-0

This book has been published with the help of a grant from the Emilio Goggio
Chair in Italian Studies, Department of Italian Studies, University of Toronto.

University of Toronto Press acknowledges the financial assistance to its publishing program of the Canada Council for the Arts and the Ontario Arts Council.

University of Toronto Press acknowledges the financial support for its publishing
activities of the Government of Canada through the Book Publishing Industry
Development Program (BPIDP).

For Robert P. Harrison,
Roberto Gonzalez Echevarria
and Philip Ewald

Contents

Foreword

This second volume in the Emilio Goggio Publication Series is by Professor Giuseppe Mazzotta, who was the Emilio Goggio Visiting Professor in the Department of Italian Studies at the University of Toronto in 1999. Incumbent of the Charles C. and Dorathea S. Dilley Chair in Italian at Yale University, he is the author of important monographs on the medieval writers Dante, Petrarch, and Boccaccio and on the eighteenth-century philosopher Vico. While at the University of Toronto during the fall term of 1999 Professor Mazzotta taught a graduate course on Boccaccio. His Goggio public lectures, grouped under the general title, 'Constructing Worlds: Renaissance Experiments,' were delivered in Alumni Hall at Victoria College on October 7, 14, and 21, 1999. They dealt with a variety of Renaissance authors, namely, Machiavelli, Ariosto, Campanella, Bacon, and Cervantes. For this volume, entitled *Cosmopoiesis: The Renaissance Experiment*, the author has supplemented the texts of his three lectures with a fourth essay on Poliziano.

My colleagues in Italian Studies and I are grateful to the members of the Goggio family for the visiting professor program that they have established in our Department. It has made possible the visits by eminent scholars and the publication of their lectures.

Olga Zorzi Pugliese
Chair, Department of Italian Studies
and Emilio Goggio Chair in Italian Studies
January 2001

Preface

It was a privilege to be asked by the Department of Italian Studies at the University of Toronto to be the Emilio Goggio Visiting Professor and to deliver the Goggio Public Lecture series in the fall of 1999. The essays here collected are largely the Goggio Lectures. They are variations on one theme: the Renaissance myth of *cosmopoiesis* or world-making. They evoke (to say it in the language of Nelson Goodman and Harry Berger) actual worlds and possible worlds, green pastoral worlds turning into scientific utopias, golden, brazen, and dreamt worlds. Above all, they focus on *making*.

A writer's world is his word or his poetic language. These essays, thus, hinge on literary constructions of the world in the period we persist in calling the Renaissance. One thread runs through the various chapters and binds them together: the theory of perspective articulated by Alberti's *Della pittura* and its prolongation in the revolutionary, even scandalous presence of Machiavelli in modern discourse. The questions that Machiavelli raises redefine the concerns of modern consciousness. We are all too familiar with his ideas. They focus on strategies for constructing the 'real' or actual world and on how power over it can be preserved. The new founders of 'real' states cannot but be sceptical about imaginary forms of world-making. They are to distrust appearances and entertain a methodical suspicion about the values of the apparent world. Because the practice of power need be either theatrical or follow secret routes, simulations and dissimulations are advisable modes of political interaction. Such realism about human passions and political morality changes the contours of modern thought. It triggers a radical rethinking of all traditional assumptions.

European thought reacts forcefully to the epochal scandal of the 'Machiavel.' The historical Machiavelli is made to put on a theatrical mask. The disguise is largely a way of exorcising the danger and diabolical prestige he represents. Other thinkers cannot but seek to gauge the new moral perspectives that Machiavelli's political-historical texts open up. In some cases, with moralistic (and suspect) ostentation, they condemn him. They are part of the tradition of the 'anti-Machiavel.' In other cases (such as those represented by Campanella and Bacon), they rethink theology, politics, ethics, and science in the light of the 'question' of power that Machiavelli puts on the front burner. They write fables wherein Plato and Machiavelli, the utopian and the actual, are brought within a single compass of concerns. On the other hand, figures such as Ariosto, Shakespeare, and Cervantes challenge the values shaping Machiavelli's actual world. They offer alternatives to the Machiavellian view of knowledge and power, and they evoke creative, possible models for the construction of new worlds.

The 'question' of which Machiavelli is the emblem marks the transition from the Middle Ages to the Renaissance. In the Middle Ages – from, say, Alan of Lille to Dante – the world is God's creation, a book written by his finger. Human beings are asked to decipher the signs of that book, often called (much as the Bible is) an *immensa sylva*. They are to sound its unfathomable depths and interpret it in the knowledge that they dwell in this world, and yet they do not belong to it. Theologians, from St Augustine to St Bonaventure and St Thomas Aquinas, speak of God's creation of the world out of nothing, how evil bursts into creation, and how the world is to be redeemed.

The Renaissance continues its extensive reflections on the poetic-theological creation of the world (Tasso, Du Bartas, Milton, and others). Giordano Bruno conjures up his vision of innumerable and infinite worlds as he rediscovers ancient Pythagorean myths of the cosmos. These philosophical, religious, and scientific cosmologies will be treated in a sustained manner in a future volume. The present essays have a narrower focus: the invention of the world and the notion of making through utopias, magic, science, art, and the theatre. These are the imaginative elements that characterize the paradigm shift from the Middle Ages to the modern age ushered in by the Renaissance. The modern world is no longer, as it was in the Middle Ages, a book that pre-exists us and whose signs we seek to decipher in the light of precepts drawn from biblical hermeneutics. The modern world, which may come through as Don Quixote's mad dream or Prospero's imaginary world that runs parallel to the actual world, is made by human art and will. It may be a labyrinth or the absolutely rational, scientific utopia drafted by Campanella and Bacon. But it is a human world, and its emblem is the work of art.

These essays will inevitably ponder the Renaissance understandings of the work of art. And they do so in both general and specific ways. The break between the Middle Ages and the Renaissance has conventionally been envisioned in somewhat different terms, which are actually coextensive with the interpretive idiom deployed here. The Middle Ages are under the sway of the *vita contemplativa*. In the Renaissance, by contrast, primacy is given to the *vita activa* or the act of making. The texts that are analysed in these essays question the rationale for positing this rupture between contemplation and action (and, consequently, between the two historical periods). They argue for the necessary interlocking of the two distinct modes of seeing and making. In order to make the world as if it were a world of art, so they tell us, we must retrieve the deeper sources of creativity that contemplation makes available. In point of fact, the very possibility of correlating making and knowing – as Alberti grasped – depends on the work of art.

The centrality of the work of art in the Renaissance not only for itself but also as a model for politics, self-making, education, and so on, hardly needs stressing. A poetic work, from *The Fable of Orpheus* to *Orlando Furioso*, is the symbolic locus where actual worlds, possible worlds, and alternative worlds are imagined and allowed to confront one another. But there is more to it. Poetry is understood in the Renaissance in a number of ways. Neoplatonists and neo-Aristotelians view it variously as a fantastic operation of the imagination (or a *mania* of the soul) as well as a production and imitation. *Téchne*, more precisely, designates the preoccupation with the rules of *poieisis* and making. At least ever since Dante, poetry is also understood in terms of the conversation of all the arts, and the term is not to be taken to signify merely the prevalence of dramatic-dialogical formal structures or the motif of *civile conversazione* or the theatre, which in truth are common aesthetic forms in the Renaissance.

In a primary way, 'conversation' defines the confrontation of world-views as well as the interaction of various disciplines or discourses, such as philosophy, history, politics, science, and literature. Within this view, no discipline is definable within its own sharply drawn borders. Each of them ceaselessly encroaches upon the other and, within the context of poetic metaphor, they mutually involve each other. More than that, poetry is considered to be unlike history and unlike philosophy. It is a fiction and knows itself to be such. Poetry's self-knowledge sets it apart from all claims of truth advanced by all other disciplines. The fiction of self-knowledge casts poetry as the ground for the conversation of the arts. Secondly, and this is true also for the Middle Ages, 'conversation' aptly describes the relation binding authors and their texts to their traditions. Much

like their texts, authors recall and answer one another across boundaries of time and space, and in the process they redesign the map of
knowledge. Finally, 'conversation' captures the mode of being of literature itself: no work of art can be grasped in isolation from the
web of relations that constitute it.

This understanding of literature as an encyclopedic conversation
both depends on and, in turn, triggers a certain way of reading. The
essays that follow stage the necessity of close reading as the preamble
to any worthwhile knowing. Reading, in this sense, is the opposite
of relying on abstract, a priori generalities about texts and the period
in which they belong. Only by focusing on the complexities of literary texts can one grasp their power to challenge the truth-value of
the various discourses – politics, ethics, science, and so on. No
doubt, by investing literature with such a privilege, one runs the risk
nowadays of appearing as if one belatedly revives residual romantic
aesthetic conceptions, as if one were speaking from the standpoint
of nostalgia for dead forms of discourse. Not for nothing, in fact,
have literary critics all but abandoned the practice of reading as if it
were a fossil. Their extra-literary concerns, however, shed little, if
any, light on the texts and are not essential to the questions put forth
by literary texts, especially those of the Renaissance. The works by a
Poliziano or Ariosto dismantle the commonplaces of contemporary
provincialism, its deluded belief (which unsurprisingly prevails
among teachers of literature) that one can do without the 'fables' of
the past. Quite to the contrary, they confirm the power of poetry
both to rethink anew the possibility of a conversation among all the
arts, to imagine and literally to make worlds that are alternative to
the actual one.

The view of Renaissance literature as the locus of making, imagining, of rhetoric, and counter-discourses was articulated by Giambattista Vico in his encyclopedic *New Science*. I recall his name for a
number of reasons. The first is that he theorized art as *poiesis* or

making and as the work of the imagination. The second reason is that he lucidly understood the Renaissance as the ambiguous time of both extraordinary achievements and inexorable decadence. The third reason is that Vico obliquely suggests how we can move beyond the limits in our current understanding of the Renaissance.

Two different interpretive strains are dominant nowadays in Renaissance scholarship. One can be called rhetorical-philological, and it stresses issues such as politics and history. The other strain, which is largely shaped by Cartesian and Hegelian (via Burckhardt) presuppositions, interprets Renaissance thought in terms of (or as a preparatory stage to) the abstract rationality of the Enlightenment. The distinction between the two paradigms is certainly not so neat, and, at any rate, Vico's way of thinking calls for moving beyond these abstract dualisms. One can do so by linking up philosophy's abstractions with philology's historical facts, politics with science, rhetoric and imagination, knowing and making.

From this Vichian critical perspective, I argue that the Renaissance texts discussed in these lectures turn against some of the predominant myths current at the time. Some of these myths come through in the lectures as particular philosophical schools – scepticism, Neoplatonism, Epicureanism, etc. The myth of making encapsulates all of them. 'Making' – this is the argument of this book – ends up disclosing, as Pico della Mirandola had seen, the Renaissance constant fascination with nothing. Its lure is compelling: The project of making is rooted in the perception of nothing. To escape this temptation, making needs to be grounded in the very mode of contemplation from which, paradoxically, modernity seeks to break away.

In closing, I wish to thank the colleagues in the Department of Italian Studies at the University of Toronto for making my visit as the 1999 Emilio Goggio Visiting Professor and lecturer so memorable and pleasant.

COSMOPOIESIS

The Renaissance Experiment

1. Poliziano's Orfeo: The World as Fable

For the carnival season of 1490 Lorenzo de' Medici wrote a *canto carnescialesco*, or carnival song, called 'La canzona di Bacco.' The song is part of the Florentine pre-Lenten festivities that were marked by songs, dances, and masked merry-making.

It is difficult to surmise what Lorenzo's song really masked. The charm of the text lies in the open celebration of youth as both a beautiful and ephemeral time: 'Quant'è bella giovinezza, / che si fugge tuttavia! / Chi vuol esser lieto, sia: / di doman non c'è certezza. / Quest'è Bacco e Arianna / belli ...' (How beautiful youth, which is ever in flight! He who so wishes, let him be merry: There is no certainty of tomorrow. These are Bacchus and Ariadne, beautiful ...).

Lorenzo's song is literally a masque or bacchanal that urges us to escape all troubles. It calls the votaries to the Epicurean/Horatian motif of *carpe diem*, to seize the moment and live in the present. Time is the carnivalesque lord of deceptions and it gives no certainty as to what tomorrow will bring. The Epicureanism of the song may well be taken to conceal Lorenzo's political manipulation of the ritual feast. Political Epicureanism, say, Lucretius's, denies any possible congruence between individual pleasures and political ends. The severance of private and public spheres is linked to another speculation developed by philosophical Epicureanism. In its rejection of astrological hermeneutics and in its positing a rational structure beneath the everyday experience of the world, Epicureanism denies knowledge of the future. Accordingly, Lorenzo's song places merriment in the present and as the feasible act of one's own will: 'chi vuol esser lieto sia.' Pleasure is both a question of one's own subjective choice and one's sense of the contingent. Within this scheme the golden age *is* the saturnalia, or, to put it differently, life is a masque, a time-bound action.

The idea of time and of uncertainty about the future, which was at the heart of this form of popular entertainment, is radically at odds with what could be called Lorenzo's politics of time or his historical sense of time. It is well known that his dynastic emblem is inscribed with the motto 'le tens revient,' 'laetus in presens,' and 'semper.' Born on January 1, Lorenzo is a Capricorn and, thus, he is under the sign of Saturn, the god of time. The frieze of his villa at Poggio a Caiano, which is decorated with a complex allegory of time, suggests that, this sense of the instability of time notwithstanding, Lorenzo envisioned a future at least for his own political dynasty.

We can never know for sure Lorenzo's political intent in his writing his carnival song, 'La canzona di Bacco,' no more than we can determine the political games he plays in writing a text such as 'La Nencia.' We do know, however, that the Saturnine, melancholy tone undergirding and unsettling the surface joy of 'Quant'è bella giovinezza' did not keep Girolamo Savonarola from opposing Lorenzo's political tyranny in Florence. He saw it as the cause of the moral decay in the city, and banned the carnival song as lewd and abhorrent. Under Savonarola's religious influence, mockeries of Lorenzo's hymn to Bacchus were written, the most memorable one being 'Il canto della morte' by Antonio Alamanni. We are on safer grounds in the knowledge that Lorenzo's poem recalls a long tradition of Dionysian songs, ranging from Ovid's *Ars Amatoria* (I, 535–62) to Poliziano's poem sung by the satyr chorus at the end of his *La fabula di Orfeo*. In many ways, as I shall argue, Lorenzo's text responds directly to the purposes of Poliziano's *La fabula di Orfeo*. The *Fabula* mixes literary and political elements and is Poliziano's 'birth of tragedy.' The tragic dismemberment of Orpheus by the Bacchants turns into the core and the point of resolution of his exploration of the myth and history.

The death of Orpheus is not the endpoint of Poliziano's narrative. The epilogue is the wild, choric 'sacrifice' by the Bacchants in honour of Bacchus. In complete forgetfulness of the violence perpetrated on Orpheus, the Bacchants sing, and their dithyramb brings the play to a close. The violent death of the individualized poet issues into a collective, rhythmic and incantatory appeal to drown the self in the voluptuous intoxication of wine. It can be inferred that for Poliziano the death of Orpheus signals the death of a certain way of doing art. It is the death of an aesthetic attitude and of a specific philosophy of harmonious order that provided the theoretical underpinning of the political myths of Lorenzo's Florence.

I shall argue, then, that the world Poliziano knew and had provisionally left behind is not a rational and coherent or harmonious world. Taken in its logical extension, the Orpheus myth celebrates and fosters an illusive and destructive order that is the death of art and of the *politeia*. To show all this, I shall focus on *La fabula di Orfeo*, on the circumstances of its composition, and on the importance of the myth of Orpheus within the intellectual climate of Poliziano's Florence. For the sake of clarity let me begin with a brief description of Poliziano's poetic itinerary.

In 1475 Poliziano wrote the *Stanze per la giostra di Giuliano de' Medici*. The notion of play and time off is at the heart of Poliziano's text, and at the heart of the game there shines the idea of beauty. The Platonic correlation of play and beauty shapes the unfolding of the poetic fragment and they are the path by which the natural world of savagery would be – in all likelihood for Poliziano – comprehended in the light of a transcendent order. The *Giostra* is literally a *ludus*, and the first stanza announces the 'fieri ludi' (fierce games) held within the city of Florence – a city, as the text has it, holding sway over all Tuscany. Giuliano appears as Iulio, which is the other name of Ascanius, and he is cast as a new Aeneas who would enter the empire of love and beauty. Poliziano will sing of Iulio: 'io canto l'amor di Iulio e l'armi,' which is a clear echo of the opening line of the *Aeneid* ('arma virumque cano'). Because it was left incomplete, we can only infer, as has been widely suggested, that the *Giostra* was conceived from the start as if it were the *Aeneid* of the Neoplatonists, as mapping, that is, the essential direction of the education of the soul. Iulio would move from the world of the hunt to the violence of nature, through the labyrinth of error, to the highest knowledge of being, what Ficino in his *Platonic Theology* calls the contemplation of one's own immortality, which is his Platonic definition of the nature of philosophy. Poliziano's poetic fragment gives only the initial phase of Iulio's spiritual process: the overcoming of nature through his encounter with beauty, embodied in Simonetta. Like play, beauty belongs to the world of phenomenal representation and glittering surfaces. Nonetheless, Simonetta's beauty awakens in Iulio the consciousness of a possible goal; it also unveils the harmony of the world which can be experienced only in a subjective dimension.

Accordingly, the text shifts direction: The blazing light of day is replaced by the world of night as it evokes the House of Sleep. The reader plunges into Iulio's imagination wherein dreams of the night are akin to and yet removed from consciousness. The essence of Poliziano's own art in the *Stanze* is to dramatize a world of playful and seductive surfaces as well as the fund of enigmas that shadow the total clarity of the daylight.

'Petrarchan' anxiety is the dimension that puts into relief the central public discourse barely sketched, but still visible in the *Stanze*. The world of play, which the Italian quattrocento had lavishly celebrated (witness the burlesque poems of Il Burchiello, the 'De iocis' of Filelfo, the *Facetiae* of Poggio, the epics of Pulci and Boiardo, the *Intercoenales* of Alberti, and the 'Nencia' of Lorenzo), opens up its power to found and celebrate within its boundaries the house of the Medici. In turn, the rational order of the city of Florence, which the Medici rule, is subjected to a Neoplatonic metaphysics of love and beauty.

It has been said in recent years that Poliziano's world is one of pure imagination and aesthetic detachment from political and moral concerns. In truth, however, Poliziano reflects on the ruptures of history. The myth of Orpheus incarnates this blend of imagination and tears in the fabric of history. Nothing shows better the reality of this claim than Poliziano's commentary on the Conspiracy of the Pazzi of April 26, 1478. This text, *Historia de Pactiona coniuratione*, is part of a commentary tradition of the tragic event that was organized to overthrow the despotism of the Medici. Unlike the commentaries by Machiavelli and Guicciardini, Poliziano's is written from the standpoint of a witness to events during which Giuliano de' Medici – the hero of the *Stanze* – is murdered by the Pazzi faction. Among the conspirators were Salviati and Bandini, two members and disciples in Ficino's Neoplatonic academy. For all the apologetic thrust of the commentary and its clear-cut contrast between, on the one hand, 'vicious conspirators,' and, on the other, the 'good' Medici household, Poliziano casts the conspiracy as a tragic spectacle and a sacrilege. It was simultaneously the profanation of the Mass and a hallowed site, and a theatre of cruelty as dismembered bodies littered the church and the streets.

The death of Giuliano was inevitably seen as an act of violence against Poliziano's own projects. It brought about the interruption of the *Stanze*. It ushered in a series of momentous changes in Poliziano's life. The changes became clear in 1480, but the signs of the changes are visible in 1479. Till that year, he had been living in the household of Lorenzo as the tutor of his oldest son, Piero, and he had been an active and cherished member of Ficino's Neoplatonic circle, the *Accademia platonica*, along with Cristoforo Landino, Pico della Mirandola, Lorenzo de' Medici, and Niccolò Machiavelli.

After the conspiracy, Lorenzo's patronage of Poliziano weakened. To contain the likely consequences of the conspiracy (such as Sforza's ambitions), Lorenzo journeyed to Naples on a diplomatic mission with the Aragonese. Poliziano had insistently asked Lorenzo to take him along, but Lorenzo refused. We do not know what had happened between them. It has been suggested that Clarice, Lorenzo's wife, a deeply religious woman, no longer wanted Poliziano to tutor her son. She probably suspected a homosexual liaison between Lorenzo and Poliziano. Or, as is likely, Savonarola's preaching was having an impact on the moral life of Florentines. To have in one's household a Hellenist, such as Poliziano (who had been translating some books of the *Iliad*), was a way of becoming the direct object of the friar's fulminations. At any rate, Poliziano left Florence and went to Mantua.

In Mantua, in the carnival season of 1480, he wrote *La fabula di Orfeo*, which marks both the beginning of Italian theatre and a new direction in Poliziano's thought. In a way, Orpheus's retrospection gives Poliziano the vantage point for his own retrospective inventory of Florentine Neoplatonism and its political applications. The Pazzi Conspiracy, which had been carried out with the complicity of some of Ficino's disciples, had two effects. It had shattered the illusion of a possible intelligible, rational political order. It had exposed the simulations in the realm of Apollinian appearances. *La fabula di Orfeo* gauges the abyss behind the illusions of order; it measures the distance between Poliziano and his friends – chief, among them, the master of Orphic mysteries, Marsilio Ficino.

The play was written in 1480 over a period of two days at the urging of Cardinal Gonzaga. Its purpose was to celebrate the marriage of Isabella d'Este and Francesco Gonzaga. But the 400 lines in the play reflect, as Vittore Branca has suggested, the impact of Aristotle's *Poetics* on Poliziano's thought. Ermolao Barbaro had just introduced him to Aristotle's *Ethics, Politics, Rhetoric,* and *Poetics.* Poliziano's Neoplatonism, however, had already been open to neo-Aristotelian influences. We know that, on the advice of Antoninus, the bishop of Florence, he had read Aquinas's *Summa contra Gentiles.* And it is also known that Ficino's metaphysics of being and creation in his *Pla-*

tonic Theology is Thomistic. Poliziano's turn to Aristotelianism was not sudden. *La fabula di Orfeo* is a trenchant critique of a wholly Neoplatonic way of looking at things.

The title, *La fabula di Orfeo*, draws the intellectual coordinates of the play. The term '*favola, fabula*' is to be taken in its etymological sense of speech (and spark of light) as a medium of philosophical doctrine. In the *Ars Poetica* (391–401), Horace speaks of the 'fable' of Orpheus taming tigers. Like the fable of Amphion, builder of Thebes, the fable of Orpheus conveys the philosophical-political wisdom/eloquence of building cities, drawing the line between public and private rights, and taming violence. In the *Poetics* of Aristotle, a fable is the *mythos* or structure of incidents. In brief, Orpheus embodies the myth of language in action, the power of language and music to awaken the will. The tradition of Orpheus the theologian and divinely inspired poet (related by Quintilian and Boethius) highlights the power of song and voice.

Son of Calliope, the muse of epic poetry, and Apollo, god of poetry who gave his son the lyre, Orpheus is linked to the union of language and music. His name means 'beautiful voice.' Indeed, accordingly, the motif of song shapes the articulation of Poliziano's text. He also grafts this primary dimension of Orpheus's mythography onto Ovid's account in the *Metamorphoses*. In Book X (1–85), Ovid tells of the death of Eurydice and of Orpheus, who mourns her. Moved by love, he dares to descend to Styx among ghosts and phantom dwellers. By the power of his chant he persuades Pluto and Persephone to let Eurydice return among the living.

At the heart of Ovid's representation of Orpheus lies the question of whether or not love – rather than confusion, fear, or harsh necessity – rules in the beyond. The story of Persephone would suggest that love presides over the silence of the vast kingdom of death. Orpheus's song casts a spell on the Furies, stops the punishments inflicted on the shades, and bends the will of Hades. Eurydice can return to life on one condition: Orpheus must not look back till he passes Avernus. When he looks back in love, Eurydice vanishes. His attempt to cross the river of death a second time is in vain. Protesting against the cruelty of the gods, Orpheus wanders alone, lives without women, and gives his love to young boys. Ovid goes on to say (*Met.* XI, 1–86) how, grieved by his rejection, the Maenads, frenzied priestesses of Bacchus, turn against Orpheus and, in their madness, scatter his limbs.

Poliziano's fable follows closely the outline of Ovid's text. Predictably – since the piece was composed in Mantua – Vergil's account of Orpheus (*Georgics* IV) is recalled. Vergil, who is an anti-Orphic poet, tells the death of Eurydice differently from Ovid. Whereas Ovid silences Aristeus's role, Vergil highlights both Aristeus's love chase and Orpheus's mad love in the loss of Eurydice. The archaeology of the myth, however, cannot completely explain Poliziano's complex manipulation. He is aware that Ficino's Neoplatonic epistemology hinges on the retrieval of the Orphic mysteries.

As D.P. Walker has documented, Ficino signs his name as 'Orpheus' in his correspondence with Poliziano.[1] Above all, he had edited the *Hymna orphica*, which are theurgic magic songs sung according to the Orphic rite. One could also say that the myth of Orpheus crystallizes Ficino's majestic design of the universe, as a glance at his *Platonic Theology* (completed in 1474) shows.

In his speculative construction of the totality of the hierarchy of creation, Ficino puts at the foundation and summit of being the divine One. A hierarchy of being – the lowest of which is corporeal matter or the domain of infinitely divisible quantity – radiates from the splendour of the One. We ascend from the materiality of existence to the domain of quality or individuated forms and to the soul (which moves matter). Above the souls are angels or perfect minds, and above the angels there is the unity of the Godhead. These levels of being are grades of power, and they are held together by bonds of sympathy. As Ficino claims later in *Three Books on Life* (written in the 1480s), a world-harmony of sympathetic attractions and accords animates and joins the degrees of creation into an aesthetic-musical cosmos.[2]

Plotinus had posited a harmony of sentient things and forces in the universe. There is an innate drawing power – he thought – in poems, songs, and prayers, and – as they vibrate – they shape the felt harmony of similar and opposite things. In the wake of Plotinus, Ficino casts music and songs as living forms or spirit: 'cantus ferme nihil aliud est quam spiritus alter' ([A] song undoubtedly is nothing else but another spirit) (*Three Books on Life*, III, 21).[3] A planetary music, composed of effluvia from above, reigns in the cosmos. From this standpoint, Ficino articulates his theory of the superiority of the sense of hearing over the other senses. Words, songs, and sounds are privileged vehicles for reaching the rational faculty of the soul. Thus, along with his father Phoebus, Orpheus is the figure of the poet who performs miracles with the enchantment of his song.

Within this dynamic and magic conception of reality (lower forms ascend to higher ones; love descends from above to creatures below, and so on), Ficino recognizes the central role played by the so-called *furores*. The term designates the four divine manias, which Plato in the *Phaedrus* identifies as the four powers of the soul. They reflect the divine force in us. In a letter, *De divino furore*, written in 1457, Ficino explains that our soul, before its descent into the body, was nourished in the contemplation of truth and beheld, as Plato has it, the justice and harmony of the divine nature. Once the soul descends into the body, it can strive to reach heaven if it is stirred by shadows and images. This striving is the divine frenzy, the vibrations in the mind refracted as the four *furores* of the soul.

The first is the *furor* of love, stirred by the appearance of beauty in the natural order. The second is the *furor* of poetry, by which the soul is led back to the memory of the celestial harmony. In the wake of Plato, who casts music and poetry as imitations of the spirit and mind of the universe, Ficino writes that 'the divine prophet Orpheus' grasped one central fact: The musical songs of the spheres – the so-called Muses – arise from Jove. The other two divine frenzies are found in the mysteries and in prophecy. The *furor* of the mysteries encompasses the worship of the gods, religious observances, and purification rites. The prophetic *furor* consists in the act of divination, in the foreknowledge inspired by the divine spirit. Ficino ends his letter by stressing that the *furores* have also false simulacra: Insane love is the false copy of divine love; superficial music is the false copy of poetry; superstition is the counterfeit of the mysteries; prediction is a caricature of prophecy.

The theory of the *furores* is restated in *De amore*, which is an exposition of Plato's *Symposium*. This series of seven dialogues, organized by Francesco Bandini, takes place on November 7 and involves, among others, Ficino, Landino, Benci, and Giovanni Cavalcanti. Their shared aim is to grasp Plato's mystical and philosophical speculations on love. Accordingly, they cast love as the principle of the whole of creation. Love staves off chaos, within which love finds itself, and it expresses itself as desire for beauty.

De amore provides also a general inventory of the themes connected with love: the passions, the two Venuses, the power of love, the hermaphrodite, the immortality of the soul, the spirituality of beauty, the relation of love to necessity (in V, xi), the role of the imagination in mediating between soul and body (in VI, vi), Guido Cavalcanti's views, and the madness of love. *De amore* comes to an end with the restatement of the four *furores* (VII, xiii) by which the soul discovers and reaches the unity of creation. The *furores* are linked with four different divinities (VII, xiv): Poetry is linked with the muses; the mysteries with Dionysius or Bacchus; divination with Apollo; and love with Venus. More poignantly, Orpheus is said to have been possessed by all four of these *furores*: 'Orfeo da tutti questi furori fu occupato;

di che li suoi libri testimonianza fanno' (Orpheus was possessed by all these frenzies. His books bear witness to it) (VII, xiv).

La fabula di Orfeo, which focuses on Orpheus's and Aristeus's love possession, on their poetic songs, on Orpheus's prophecy, and the final Bacchic mysteries, grapples squarely with Ficino's fundamental question: the ambiguities of the *furores* and their problematical relationship to death or immortality. Seeing Poliziano at odds with Ficino is not unusual. It was one of Pico della Mirandola's followers, Juan-Luis Vives, who suggested that Poliziano was unlike Ficino or Pico. By making reference to the *Centuriae*, Poliziano, so Vives says, is a philologist and a grammarian bent on deciding the right spelling of 'Vergilius' or 'Virgilius.' Poliziano is even accused by Vives of holding Scripture in contempt. On the other hand, Ficino and Pico saw Scripture as the resting point of all the arts. According to Vives, they were disgusted by all other writings.

Vives's partiality toward Ficino and Pico is understandable, but is not accurate. After all, his *Fable about Man* (*Fabula de homine*), which pulls together the strands of Cusanus's *De ludo globi* and Pico's *De dignitate hominis*, claims that man's divinity resides in his ability to play. Play, as Plato knew, is the mark of man's nobility, by which he can ceaselessly invent himself and, chameleon-like, take on an infinity of roles. Yet, Vives's dismissal of Poliziano's philology as pure pedantry misses the point. From Poliziano's perspective, Vives, as much as Ficino or Pico, with their schemes of the unbroken chain of causality linking God and the natural world, did not understand historical reality. Poliziano's historical sense – embodied by his philology and his awareness of Florentine politics as a demonic possession – leads him to question the grand metaphysical frameworks that obliterate history. *La fabula di Orfeo* is the critical narrative of Poliziano's scepticism toward Ficino's optimistic belief in harmony, his theory that the essence of reality can be controlled by the magic powers of Neoplatonic rationality.

The play opens with Mercury, god of speech, laws, and psychopomp, leading the shades to Hades. The presence of the god marks a shift from the conventions of sacred representations to a secular concern. The change of direction inaugurates a tragic world. It adumbrates Poliziano's pursuit of a new art, the art of music and poetry, in order to probe the tragic nature of Renaissance humanism and Florentine Hellenism. Mercury's speech announces the 'festa.' The term defines the representation itself as a ludic action. More substantively, the speech recalls Apollo and Aristeus, who loved Eurydice with 'sfrenato ardore' (unbridled desire).

The reference to Aristeus's desire as transgressive of boundaries leads to a pastoral scene that is modelled – predictably, given the Mantuan context of the performance – on Vergil's *Eclogues* and *Georgics*. But Poliziano alters the tradition. The idyllic pastoral tradition evokes an ideal world of nature that is constructed on the false premise of man's possible mastery of nature. In this sense, the pastoral world blazes trails that later scientific projects of utopias (i.e., Campanella's *City of the Sun* and Bacon's *New Atlantis*) will take. The pastoral representation of nature, however, runs the risk of trivializing the natural world by the optimistic view of man's power over it.

In Poliziano's pastoral landscape there is no harmony. There are discordant voices and viewpoints. The old shepherd Mopsus, who stands for the pastoral ethics of containment of desire, has lost his calf and asks Aristeus if he has seen it. Aristeus replies as if he were Iulio in the *Stanze*: He has seen a nymph more beautiful than Diana and is possessed by a love mania.

Poliziano, in effect, asks what the pastoral always (if implicitly) asks: What is man's place in nature? The question presupposes that we know what nature is. For Mopsus, the pastoral describes a world where there is a place for everything and everything should be in its place. He endorses the implications of the *humble style*: Man can have mastery over animals. Within this worldview, one can control lower beings as well as the troubled, inner world of desire. Mopsus's moral certitudes are grounded in humility. He asks questions about a lost calf and has an answer for Aristeus's desire (he should flee from it). His humility cannot account for Aristeus's passion for beauty. Thus Mopsus's version of the pastoral marks the death of the imagination. Nonetheless, Aristeus's imaginative desire or uncontrolled *furor* has its own self-deception.

Aristeus's underlying belief is that the unbounded natural world is his place. He cannot imagine, therefore, the indifference of nature to his love pangs. The song he sings ('Udite, selve, mie dolce parole / poi che la ninfa mia udir non vole' [Hear, woods, my sweet words since my nymph does not want to hear them]) unfolds the *carpe diem* motif ('la mia vita fugge via' [my life flees fast away]) as a ploy to seduce Eurydice. The song, however, does not bend Eurydice. Aristeus is a deluded, Petrarchan lover. He rejects Mopsus's ethos of containment and believes in the power of song to establish a harmonious bond between himself and nature. He believes language can conjure up the world as he wishes it to be. He does not really grasp the nature of the love that possesses his mind.

During his chase of Eurydice, he wishes Love would give him wings to catch up with her. But he is unaware of the Platonic resonance of his language: His love is not the Platonic mania leading up the ladder of being. His love quest remains within the horizontal plane of the 'selve,' a term Cristoforo Landino glosses as the embodiment of materiality. Further, Aristeus's love ravishes his mind, 'mente' (l. 31). In Ficino's lexicon, the word describes the highest part of the soul (the other two are *ratio* and *phantasia*). Aristeus's mind, instead, pursues vanishing phantasms.

The whole pastoral world reveals itself as a deluded fiction in Poliziano's representation. Its assumption of order is wishful thinking. Tirsi, Mopsus's servant, has been looking for the lost calf and finally finds it. The violence of the language ('così gli avess'io el collo mozzo') [would that I had cut its throat (94)] looks forward to the violence of the Dionysian ritual at the end of the play. It unveils the shepherds' mastery over the natural world as an exercise of violence.

In contrast to the turbulence and disorder beneath the seductive simplicities of the pastoral surface of the natural world, there is the world of Orpheus. He appears singing and playing on the lyre. The stage direction places us in the world of the court. We are told that Orpheus's song in Latin is meant for Poliziano's new patron, Cardinal Gonzaga. Orpheus's *carmen* (meaning both song and oracle) is unlike his earlier *lusus*, the playful love games of Aristeus's idyllic interlude. It is as if the pastoral were a false aesthetic game.

Orpheus's new song is vatic and it stems from Apollo, the god of prophecy:

> an vati bonus haec canenti dictat Apollo?
> Phoebe, quae dictas rato fac precamur. (152–4)

> [Am I at fault, or doth a kindly Apollo inspire the bard who thus sings?
> Phoebus, bring thou to fulfilment, we pray, thine inspiration.][4]

The Apollinian world, which is also Aristeus's world, accounts for Orpheus's prophetic-political voice. Like the Mantuan prophet Ocnus, who founded the city of Mantua, Orpheus wishes to usher in a new political order. The augury is that the Gonzaga household may be visited by the horn of plenty; that this house may know a new efflorescence of art; and that the cardinal be made pope in the not so distant future. In short, the prophetic-divinatory song conjures up a new world. The divination concerns, transparently enough, the Medici household, and its pursuit of poetic-political laurels. The prophecy is interrupted by the sudden news of Eurydice's death.

With her death, the text abandons all Apollinian illusions and shifts to a Dionysian tragic mode. Poetry is now the performer and its claims of power move centre stage as Orpheus confronts and seeks to overcome, by his voice and music, the power of death. If nature is ruled by death and the laws of necessity, Orpheus is engaged in an unnatural quest. He wills to transgress the laws of necessity and all ideas of limit to the poetic enterprise.

To highlight the uniqueness of Orpheus's poetic *furor*, which brings him to the heart of death, the text evokes, at its exact numerical centre, the tragic myth of Philomela (201). In Ovid's account, she was violated by Tereus and had her tongue cut off. The threat of the possible silencing of the poetic voice turns into the conviction, which is central to Poliziano's thought, that poetic language (as his introduction to Quintilian has it) is the portal of access to the soul of human beings. It constitutes the fabric of the world; it has the power to disrupt – as Vergil's *Georgics* IV has it – the order of nature.

By a reversal of the earlier language of Aristeus, Orpheus is said to have reached the gates of Hell on the 'wings of love' (217). His downward flight placates the fury ('furore') (218) of Cerberus. Orpheus's descent of love, no doubt, acknowledges one of Ficino's insights into Platonic love. Whereas Plato views love as the dialectical movement of the mind upward, Ficino stresses both the ascent and the descent of love. This downward motion of love captures the Christian dimension that Ficino adds to classical philosophy.

Orpheus's song to Pluto is predicated on the Ficinian premise that music soothes the perturbations of the soul and unifies all discordant strains in creation. 'The Platonists say,' Ficino writes, 'that the force itself of a thing, almost a certain life of it, is hidden in the form of this voice, word, or name, which comprises its articulate parts' (*Epitome of Plato's Cratylus*). The force of sound, he adds, comes forth through *orationes*, *incantationes*, and *invocationes*. Accordingly, Orpheus's song bends Proserpina's will because it is a song and a prayer: 'canto, per l'amor pe' giusti prieghi' (293). In so far as the song enacts an extended reflection on nature, it departs from Ficino's representation of nature.

Orpheus's song is a cosmological song. It evokes the world of nature as the realm of necessity and death. In this circle of imma-nence, everything stems from chaos and returns to death. But there is still Ficinian love even in the dark abyss of death. Pluto's assent to Orpheus's triumph over death – to the immortality of Orpheus – signals that love conquers death. But Orpheus, who has transgressed all laws and who stands for transgression itself, unavoidably trans-gresses the injunction not to look back at Eurydice and loses her.

Orpheus's impatient retrospection presupposes a freedom of action, the assertion of a choice above and beyond the constraints of necessity. It shows that Orpheus forever transgresses all laws and boundaries. The loss of Eurydice, however, convinces Poliziano, against Ficino, that we are not in an anthropocentric cosmos and that men, including Orpheus, occupy a subordinate role in it. What is more, human passions – or the *furores* – are not univocal, as Ficino thinks they are. Ficino's theoretical and optimistic rationalism casts them as spiritual-phantasmatic vehicles of the transcendence of empirical reality. Poliziano, by contrast, centres on the wild, destruc-tive energy of the *furores*, and their terrifying, uncontainable power to annihilate Orpheus. What eludes Ficino's intellectual Apollinian effort is the tragic depth of the Greek myth: the ugly discordance at the heart of the process of life.

Twice the text registers the destructiveness of the *furores*: Eurydice is lost by a 'furore': 'ti son tolta a gran furore' (308). Orpheus echoes her language: 'O mio furore' as a Fury opposes his attempted second *katabasis* into Hell. Poliziano's critique of Ficino, moreover, invests the political Neoplatonism of Florence, of which Ficino was the court theorist. Among the audience at Ficino's lectures on Plato – as is known – there was Machiavelli as well as some of the conspirators against the Medici, such as Salviati and Bandini. Retrospectively,

Ficino's metaphysics of light hid the sinister shadows of conspiracy. It could no longer appear to be a serene rationale for Lorenzo's rule. The dramatic action of the play shatters all likely optimism. Orpheus, anguished over his defeat by the powers of death, roams over the fields and chooses the unnatural love of boys. By the final transgression of the laws of nature he locks himself into himself. Mad at the contempt Orpheus shows for the 'teda legittima' (legitimate union), the Maenads perform a Dionysian ritual and tear him apart. His sacrificial death (line 369) recalls Ficino's *De sacrificio* (a translation of Proclus's Neoplatonic text). For Poliziano, 'sacrificio' designates the last of the four *furores*, the ecstatic mysteries of Dionysian wild orgies. More to the point, the frenzy of the Bacchants textually recalls Poliziano's own account of the Pazzi conspiracy.

La fabula di Orfeo features characters who never confront each other. Each character is alone. The series of lyrical 'Petrarchan' monologues punctuating the text betray the solipsistic thrust of the play. In the pastoral world the voices of Aristeus and Mopsus are self-answerable. Orpheus sings monologues or addresses death. By contrast, the chorus of the Bacchants at the end is not individualized. It is addressed to all. It exists as an undifferentiated group joined together by virtue of the *furor* emanating from the religious mystery.

The end of the play features a drunken speech. The incantation by the crowd celebrates the world as dance and as an affirmation of joy and life. In this communal *furor*, the legal-political ethos of moderation and restraint is abandoned. The enthusiastic worshippers are intoxicated with Dionysus, who is traditionally *demotikos* and *lusios*, god of the people and liberator of instincts. The supreme ecstasy of the zealots annihilates the individual; it shows the legalistic order of Pluto giving way to the chaos of the Bacchants. Orpheus shuttles between these poles of experience and dies.

Is there a difference between Orpheus's transgressive values and the practice of the Bacchants? Or between Apollo and Dionysus? There are differences, and they are of degree. Orpheus stands for the despotic transgression of all limits. His desire, which expresses the desire to be otherwise, at first comes through as a defence of love and life, and ends up as a dithyramb of death. On the other hand, the chorus of the Bacchants acknowledges Bacchus as the guide everyone is to follow: 'Ognun segua Bacco / eu oè.'

There is an inscription at Eleusis: *Dionisos Parapaison* – Dionysus lover of the game. The Dionysian feast in Poliziano's text turns into delirium. The sacred play of the Maenads – made of wine, music, song, and dances – is changed into a drunken song. Inarticulate sounds ('eu,' 'oè') counterfeit harmony; Epicurean pleasure hides violence; the language violates grammatical norms (with forms such as 'bever,' 'mi,' 'ti,' and others) evoking the stylistics of the humble pastoral world. The unindividualized multitude misunderstands the unsteady tottering engendered by wine as a dance pattern.

Lorenzo de' Medici, who was called the 'needle' on the scale of Italian politics, saw politics as a dance or economy of checks and balances. Poliziano's *La fabula di Orfeo* – made of formal symmetries, weights and counterweights – unveils the limitations of both the politics and the philosophical-poetic myths that surround Lorenzo's politics. The myth of Orpheus involves Ficino, Lorenzo, and Poliziano himself.

In the carnival song of 1490, Lorenzo responds to Poliziano's pessimism. The provisional carnivalesque disorder is a mask of a musical-political orchestration that is manipulated by the invisible hand of the Prince. This was, after all, the burden of 'La Nencia.' But Lorenzo was wrong. Savonarola's attacks against the Medici show that he had pierced the mask of the political manipulation of art, to which he was to oppose a new, moral aesthetics.

It is commonly said that Lorenzo's circle dissolved in the 1490s.

The break between Ficino, on the one hand, and Pico and Benivi-
eni, on the other, is a sign of the dissolution. So is the critique of
paganizing Neoplatonism unleashed by Savonarola against Ficino.
La fabula di Orfeo is the sober divination of the imminent crisis. By
the drunkenness in the final scene, it narrates that foundations shake
and that we are no longer in the firm land of understanding. It
recalls a myth that plunges us into a world of evanescent shadows. It
tells of transgressions and violence that eerily resemble the violence
of the historical world.

In effect, *La fabula di Orfeo* marks the emergence of the world as a
fable, the world as a language construction. This is not Poliziano's
way of denying the empirical world and of asserting that history
exists only in the mind. In this tale, there is no rift between the 'real'
world and the 'fictional' world. As Petrarch had done with the 'fable'
of his own self, Poliziano writes a text in which history and imagination overlap: Each reaches into the other, each is the dream and the
truth of the other. As it does so, the fable looks dreamily forward to
a time when the 'Aristotelian,' rational, realistic mode of thought
and aesthetics – such as the one Florence knew with Leonardo Bruni
– would become, at least as wishful thinking, the basis of a new
politics.

Eventually, Poliziano would return to Florence. He taught Greek
in the Studium there and produced his philological works. His interlocutor was Savonarola and, when he died in 1494, he asked to be
buried in the habit of the Dominicans. He ended up sympathizing
with the friar's theocratic utopia that was soon to burn to ashes.
Machiavelli, however, thought otherwise.[5]

2. Ariosto and Machiavelli: Real Worlds / Imaginary Worlds

The last canto of *Orlando Furioso* (XLVI) opens with a memorable scene. The poet's boat is finally gliding ashore and the dazzling whirligig of his imagination goes around one more time. Most, but by no means all, of the glamorous ladies, legendary princes and courtiers, distinguished men and women of letters of the time – Aretino, Sannazaro, Vittoria Colonna, Veronica Gambara, and others – are waiting on the waterfront to cheer the poet's triumphant return from his marvellous wanderings.

The poet's digression on this imaginary return is brief. In terms of the narrative movement the vignette is meant both to highlight and counter the depth of violence into which the final canto will soon plunge us and which culminates with Rodomonte's death. In and of itself, the welcoming scene recalls the legendary names of the Italian Renaissance. The enumeration of pure names, which faintly recalls Petrarch's 'Triumph of Fame,' casts the poem as the social register of the Renaissance, and it casts the Renaissance as a brilliant and yet frivolous theatre. It is also the poet's fantasy of social recognition; because the list of names is not all-inclusive, it may even be taken as a spoof of the game played by polite society of counting who is in and who is out at the party.

One reader of *Orlando Furioso* was not amused at being overlooked by Ariosto, and he actually felt slighted by the oversight. In a letter to Lodovico Alamanni of December 17, 1517, Machiavelli, who had just finished reading Ariosto's epic, admits being delighted by the poem but voices his regrets at being left out of this Renaissance hall of fame.

We can understand, perhaps even sympathize with Machiavelli's personal disillusionment at not being acknowledged by Ariosto – just one more disillusionment for a man who knows he deserves better and who feels scorned from all sides. Yet Machiavelli's complaint is more than just a personal peeve. Machiavelli is everywhere in the *Furioso*. In point of fact, *Orlando Furioso* reformulates the key features of Machiavelli's vision but offers a deeply divergent alternative. Thus, it won't do to seek to justify the omission of Machiavelli's name, as critics of good will try to do, in narrowly philological terms of sifting the evidence as to how much or how little Ariosto had read of Machiavelli. *Orlando Furioso* would be neither possible nor necessary apart from Machiavelli's political scheme. In the following pages I shall show the extent of Ariosto's involvement with the intellectual perspectives and presuppositions of his time; in his dialogue with his contemporaries, Machiavelli is always present, yet he can't but be left behind.

The common point of departure for Ariosto and Machiavelli is the overriding, fundamental question of power, which haunts the imagination of the Renaissance, and which had been relentlessly probed by almost everyone of consequence. Machiavelli is the figure who epitomizes this concern. Simply put, for Machiavelli everything is drawn within the inexorable orbit of power and is shaped by it. The proposition is hardly new, but Machiavelli gave it a fresh twist.

In the Middle Ages power belongs to a sacred order. A spiritual mythology shrouds power, justifies it, and gives prestige to its exercise. The mechanism is simple: power is said to emanate from God and to trickle down to the finite realm of creatures. The conciliar debates on the *plenitudo potestatis* (fullness of power) – Marsilius of Padua's critique of papal power (whether or not power ought to reside in the *universitas fidelium*, the bishops, or the sole authority of the Pope), and the secular, legal claims for the Emperor's *potestas suprema mundi* (absolute earthly power) – all reaffirm, even as they debate how it has to be parcelled out, the mystical and sacred origins of power.

Machiavelli's *The Prince* brushes off at the start the notion of the supernatural essence of power; it demythologizes the belief in the magic or sacred origin of power; it brings power within the bounds and imaginative grasp of man and shows its illusory contrivances.

Moses, for instance, is for Machiavelli not a religious leader or the cabalistic figure treading esoteric paths of knowledge. Like Cyrus, Theseus, and Romulus, Moses embodies the quality of supremely skillful political leadership. There is undoubtedly a great irony in making Moses a model of political success, for Moses never reached the promised land and it was left to Joshua to do so. Moses' failure in effect casts an unmistakably ironic light on the portrait of the prince, for it implies that, like Moses, he is a figure whose projects fall short of being realized. More to the point, the interpretive twist in the representation of Moses signals Machiavelli's moral will to read power in purely secular terms.

Machiavelli's desacralized, rational (and, from this viewpoint, moral) understanding of power (which later both Bacon and Vico were to endorse) also steers clear of the organization and containment of power made available by imaginary utopias, from Plato's *Republic* to More's *Utopia*. Chapter XV of *The Prince* addresses the radical inadequacies of intellectual utopian creations and dismisses them:

> Ma sendo l'intento mio scrivere cose utile a chi la intende, mi è parso più conveniente andare drieto alla verità effettuale della cosa, che alla imaginazione di essa. E molti si sono imaginati repubbliche e principati che non si sono mai visti né conosciuti essere in vero; perché egli è tanto discosto da come si vive a come si doverrebbe vivere, che colui che lascia quello che si fa per quello che si doverrebbe fare impara piuttosto la ruina che la perservazione sua: ... Lasciando, adunque, indrieto le cose circa uno principe imaginate, e discorrendo quelle che sono vere, dico che ...

> [But since my intention is to write something useful for anyone who understands it, it seemed more suitable to me to search after the effectual truth of the matter rather than its imagined one. And many

writers have imagined for themselves republics and principalities that
have never been seen nor known to exist in reality; for there is such a
gap between how one lives and how one ought to live that anyone
who abandons what is done for what ought to be done learns his
ruin rather than his preservation: ... Leaving aside, therefore, the
imagined things concerning a prince, and taking into account those
that are true, I say that ...][1]

This rejection of utopian visionariness is tantamount to a refusal
of utopias' underlying ethical imaginings – the refusal to see, for
instance, how justice, which is unavoidably the scandal of political
practice, can be related to the realities of power. Finally, the casting
of utopias as pure fiction without basis in fact is the flip side of
Machiavelli's grounding of power in the solid reality of the historical
record.

Ironically, however, Machiavelli, for all his political realism, cannot escape constructing a new and more frightening demonology of
power in the very act in which *The Prince* maps and recounts past
experiences of power as possible strategies for its acquisition. Because power in *The Prince* is value-free, purposeless, and nontele-
ological, it comes forth as a never-ending drive that becomes concrete in the encounter of conflicting wills. More specifically, the
metaphysical foundation of Machiavelli's world is the disorder of
a fallen state of nature; the principles of this condition of existence
are force and simulation – the traits, respectively, of the lion and the
fox – whereby power is acquired and retained.

From this perspective of simulation, power entails that it be per-
fectly visible, for its substance, paradoxically, is determined by the
appearance of power. Hence its emphasis on spectacles and ceremo-
nies of power; on the staging of exemplary actions, such as public
executions, in the public square for all to see and be intimidated by;
on manipulating appearances (the prince, we are told, must *seem*

pious, and *seeming* pious is preferable to *being* pious). In *The Prince* the idea of the magic origin of power is refuted from a rational standpoint; yet the world of simulacra takes over and reality grows dim while the prince, as if he were a real sorcerer, turns into the lord of appearances, tricks, and illusions. This vision of history in terms of the black magic of power, with power as source and aim of all endeavours, appeared unfeasible to Machiavelli's friend Guicciardini, who judged and dismissed Machiavelli's abstract and absolute convictions from the viewpoint of his daily engagement in the tough games of political compromise. It also seemed unrealistic to utopian thinkers, like Campanella, who elaborated a more thorough theory of natural law than the truncated version that Machiavelli upheld.

But Machiavelli's power-centred vision seems to be inadequate when viewed from the perspective of Ariosto or from that of the Elizabethan stage. From their perspective, in fact, it would seem that Machiavelli has a tragic sense of the nature of power but that he is unable to transcend it. It is no accident that the Elizabethan stage – Marlowe, Shakespeare, and others – steadily presents Machiavelli as a tragic figure akin to Faustus and Tamburlaine. What is equally remarkable, I believe, is that it is as a tragic text that Machiavelli himself understands *The Prince*.

There is no possible umbrella definition of *tragedy* in the Renaissance, for it knew and produced too many and too disparate versions of tragedies. I will thus explain what I mean by the term as I go along. It can be easily agreed that the primary impulse of *The Prince* is the quest for a hero who would act on the disjointed realities of Italian history and who would give a single purpose to power, which at the time kept drifting into a variety of competing directions. In contrast to the anarchic particularisms of rivalling interests, the prince is he who would create and conjure up a generalized political organism by the sheer power and force of his will. There are no limits to what this waited-for hero can do; the prince, who is certainly not a prince of peace, is free to act; indeed, he is summoned to heroic action, while the constraints on him are never moral.

This configuration of the large compass of the prince's *virtù* is unquestionable. There is, however, another side to this assumption of the prince's sphere of action. Whatever happens, Machiavelli steadily tells us, happens of necessity; the efforts to shape the contingent randomness of Fortune are always likely to be defeated; in brief, the world is never the direct outcome of our schemes and designs on it. Chapter 25 of *The Prince* lucidly focuses on the irreducibility of the scheme of things to the thoughts of man:

Nondimanco, perché il nostro libero arbitrio non sia spento, iudico poter esser vero che la fortuna sia arbitra della metà delle azioni nostre, ma che etiam lei ne lasci governare l'altra metà, o presso, a noi. E assomiglio quella a uno di quei fiumi rovinosi, che, quando s'adirano, allagano e' piani, ruinano gli alberi e gli edifizi, lievono da questa parte terreno, pongono da quell'altra; ciascuno fugge loro dinanzi, ognuno cede allo impeto loro, sanza potervi in alcuna parte obstare. E benché sieno così fatti, non resta però che gli uomini, quando sono tempi quieti, non vi potessino fare provvedimenti e con ripari e argini, in modo che, crescendo poi, o egli andrebbano per uno canale, o l'impeto loro non sarebbe né sì licenzioso né sì dannoso. Similmente interviene della fortuna; la quale dimostra la sua potenzia dove non è ordinata virtù a resisterle; e quivi volta li sua impeti dove la sa che non sono fatti gli argini e li ripari a tenerla.

[Nevertheless, in order that our free will not be extinguished, I judge it to be true that Fortune is the arbiter of half of our actions, but that she still leaves the control of the other half, or almost that, to us. And I compare her to one of those ruinous rivers that, when they become enraged, flood the plains, and tear down the trees and buildings, taking up earth from one spot and placing it upon another; everyone flees from them; everyone yields to their onslaught, unable to oppose them in any way. And although they are of such a nature, it does not follow that when the weather is calm we cannot take precautions with embankments and dikes, so that when they rise up again either the waters will be channeled off or their impetus will not be either so disastrous or so damaging. The same things happen where Fortune is concerned: she shows her force where there is no organized strength to resist her; and she directs her impact there where she knows that dikes and embankments are not constructed to hold her.] (p. 159)

There is an overt imbalance between man's will and the capricious, forever shifty dominion of Fortune. The powerful metaphor of the river and the bank, which is Dantesque in origin and which Shakespeare also employs, illustrates Machiavelli's understanding of the relation between man and the inscrutable Goddess Fortuna. Later in the text this relationship will be presented in misogynistic terms of wife beating. But the image of the river at this juncture conveys the tragic vision of man's impossible but unavoidable effort to contain and control the vital powers of nature. Man will shore up the bank to hold off the fury of the flood, and yet the waters will certainly break loose again. What gives tragic grandeur to this experience is Machiavelli's conviction of man's necessary, at once heroic and futile (and heroic because futile) countereffort in the face of certain defeat. From this perspective *The Prince* can be said to straddle the boundaries of two rhetorical genres: It is both a text of absolute political action and an aesthetic representation of the failure to carry out political plans and visions.

The Elizabethans perceived *The Prince's* logical link between the aesthetics of gratuitous, absolute, amoral action and the irresistible lure of power, and the link constituted the tragic core of their stage representation of the Machiavel. Other readers never nuanced their judgment and fiercely objected to Machiavelli's trenchant figuration of the blind force of power. The most notorious among these readers are also the most suspect: They are the polemicists in the tradition of the anti-Machiavel (represented, ironically enough, by baroque theorists of absolute power – Gentile, Bodin, Botero, Boccalini, and others), who understood, probably too well, that a truly Machiavellian posture is to profess anti-Machiavellianism. But Machiavelli's idea of power stems from the critical perspective of the Stoics. Ariosto refocuses on the question of the origin and essence of power, as Machiavelli did, but, unlike Machiavelli, Ariosto will delineate the movement by which the imagination will undercut the power of power.

I shall illustrate Ariosto's critique of power by looking, to begin with, at one detail of his epic: its title, *Orlando Furioso*. The title, as is known, is primarily a takeoff from the earlier and highly successful *Orlando Innamorato* by Boiardo. But it also alludes, as is also widely known, to the title of one of Seneca's tragedies, *Hercules furens*. Why would Hercules be important for Ariosto's imagination? What are the semantic extensions of *furens*? And why would Seneca be a notable point of reference for Ariosto's epic? Who is, in brief, Seneca in the Renaissance? To begin to answer these questions one may look at the opening stanzas of *Orlando Furioso*:

> Le donne, i cavallier, l'arme, gli amori,
> le cortesie, l'audaci imprese io canto,
> che furo al tempo che passaro i Mori
> d'Africa il mare, e in Francia nocquer tanto,
> seguendo l'ire e i giovanil furori
> d'Agramante lor re, che si diè vanto
> di vendicar la morte di Troiano
> sopra re Carlo imperator romano.

Dirò d'Orlando in un medesmo tratto
cosa non detta in prosa mai né in rima:
che per amor venne in furor e matto,
d'uom che sì saggio era stimato prima;
se da colei che tal quasi m'ha fatto,
che il poco ingegno ad or ad ora mi lima,
me ne sarà però tanto concesso,
che mi basti a finir quanto ho promesso.

Piacciavi, generosa Erculea prole,
ornamento e splendor del secol nostro,
Ippolito, aggradir questo che vuole
e darvi sol può l'umil servo vostro. (I, 1–3)

[Of ladies, cavaliers, of love and war
Of courtesies and of brave deeds I sing
In times of high endeavour when the Moor
Had crossed the sea from Africa to bring
Great harm to France, when Agramante swore
In wrath, being now the youthful Moorish king,
To avenge Troiano, who was lately slain,
Upon the Roman Emperor Charlemagne.

And of Orlando I will also tell
things unattempted yet in prose or rhyme,
Of the mad frenzy that for love befell
One who so wise was held in former time,
If she who my poor talent by her spell
Has so reduced that resemble him,
Will grant me now sufficient for my task:
The wit to reach the end is all I ask.

Most generous and Herculean son,
The ornament and splendour of our age,
Ippolito, pray take as for your own
Your humble servant's gift, that men may gauge
The debt I owe to you ...][2]

The opening two lines of the first stanza of the poem list the variety of themes – women, knights, loves, courtesies, and adventures – that constitute the tangled strands of the text. The nouns listed in sequence, as Carne-Ross noted some years ago, are all in the plural, as if to convey the plurality of experiences as well as the epic all-inclusiveness of life Ariosto pursues.[3] More substantively, the first *ottava* evokes the epic war between Christians and Moslems, the siege of Paris at the time of Charlemagne. The war, which is a central concern of the epic vision and of this epic in particular, is said to be the outcome of Agramante's 'furori' – literally, furies – madness and rage.

The second ottava marks a radical shift from the world of war to the world of love. It shifts, to say it more accurately, from the *outside*, public domain of war as a spiral of violence and revenge to the *inner*, private world of Orlando's madness, which is called – in a symmetrical balance to Agramante's 'furori' – 'furore.' In another oblique parallel to the disorder of Orlando's mind there is a reference to the poet's own 'poco ingegno' or small wit. The poet, in effect, who is always inside the story (and has been, like so many of his characters, voyaging over uncharted imaginary spaces) and who is also outside of the story (manipulating the intricate threads of his text), casts himself as a naive figure at the edge of the facts to be narrated.

The symmetrical reference to the ravages of the war and to the rage in the landscape of the hero's mind is followed by the poet's *captatio benevolentiae*. The poet addresses his patron, Ippolito d'Este, who is said to be the descendant of Hercules. The apostrophe discloses the chief political theme of *Orlando Furioso* as well as the more general imaginative concerns of the epic. Every epic tells essentially what can be called the central Machiavellian myth of the city: how new cities are founded and old ones are destroyed, how empires are established and are given legitimacy. *Orlando Furioso*, accordingly, is the narrative of the establishment of a dynasty, the Este family, from the marriage of a heroine, Bradamante, to Ruggiero, a Moslem who converts to Christianity. The mythography of Hercules – his process of education, his civilizing role in, say, his victory over Cacus – shapes and adumbrates a large and crucial portion of the poem: the education of the weak-willed Ruggiero, to put it in the terms of one of Erasmus's works, as a Christian prince. But there are other elements in the mythography of both Hercules and Hyppolitus that are primary in Ariosto's moral imagination. These elements are to be found in two tragic texts of Seneca: *Hercules furens* and *Hyppolitus*.

Hyppolitus is the tragic account of hapless Phaedra's passion for her stepson, Hyppolitus. Her love is madness, a fever that parches her soul. For Seneca, more precisely, Phaedra's lust, which brings destruction to both Hyppolitus and Phaedra herself, is a war of the mind, for in this text Venus is coupled with Mars. *Hercules furens*, on the other hand, has its point of departure in the mythic tradition of *Hercules invictus*, the invincible hero who has successfully accomplished the twelve mighty tasks imposed on him by the wrath of Juno. When the last of his labours is completed and Hercules returns from Hades to the upper world with Cerberus, Hercules goes mad. The triumph over death has just been accomplished, but it is now thwarted as day turns to night: Hercules is powerless to repress the mad fury of his heart and is overcome by horrible imaginings. He mistakes his own children for those of the king and kills them.

The two Senecan texts can be best understood within the framework of Stoic theories of the passions. Like Cicero (especially in the *Tusculanae* [3, 7] and *De finibus* [3, 35]), like Epictetus and Marcus Aurelius, Seneca views the passions – grief, fear, pleasure, and anger, that which the Greeks call *pathe* and the Romans *perturbationes* or *morbi* – as diseases one should avoid. Seneca, who had to deal with Caligula and in vain sought to educate Nero, knew well that the outside, public world is full of snares and dangers. The Stoic sage, therefore, is he who keeps his soul free, lives in self-sufficiency and follows the laws of nature. The sage, in short, must cultivate apathy, which is not callous indifference; it is, rather, the virtue of imperturbability, the rational choice of resisting the motions and impulses (*horme*) of the excited mind. To this moral end of self-control and spiritual freedom, Seneca's treatise *On Providence* recommends avoiding luxury as an injurious excess and shunning prosperity, 'which affects the brain, conjures empty fantasies up in the mind, and befogs the distinction between true and false with a confusing cloud.' Tranquillity of mind or *euthymia* (literally, the well-being of the soul), Seneca says in his treatise quoting Democritus, can be attained by not engaging in many activities, private or public, and by removing oneself from the pursuit of the goods that are under the power of fortune.[4]

What Seneca and the Stoics fully grasp is exactly the truth that Machiavelli did not understand but Ariosto lucidly understood. The power over others that *The Prince* pursues has its own irresistible fascination. But for Ariosto, who follows Seneca in this, the pursuit into the outside world is madness, *furor*, the implacable force unlocking the grim gates of war. The limit in Machiavelli's figuration of power lies in his placing the turbulence and strife only in the outside world, which the prince would have to channel and shape into the work of art. There is a stronger power inside the self, and this is identifiable with the passions that force one to act, with the dizziness and disorder within the mind. Orlando, like Hercules, is the hero who conquers all but succumbs to the treacherous figments of his own mind. Following Seneca, in short, power for Ariosto is not simply what is visible on the stage of Machiavellian politics; rather, he probes the enigma of the passions that underlie and shape the actions of the hero.

The internalized passion that moves Orlando and all the other paladins in *Orlando Furioso* is love, a demon that is never in our power and that actually overpowers us, even as it empowers one to act. In the epic, more specifically, love has also to be understood in terms of the humoral pathology of the passions. The semantic extension of the Latin word *furor* is melancholy or black bile, which, as the Neoplatonist Ficino writes in his *De vita triplici*, can be a divine frenzy (*divinum furorem*) inducing philosophical speculations, ravings, and lethargy. In other words, *Orlando Furioso* already contains in itself *Orlando Innamorato*, for love brings to the fore the madness that lies hidden, like a secret passion or an obstinate temptation, within the fantasies of love.

Orlando appears from the very start as a Petrarchan lover, fascinated with Angelica, who is forever in flight. He dresses in black, because he is the *chevalier noir* of French romances, and because black is the colour of melancholy. In his single-minded pursuit of the inaccessible and often invisible woman, Orlando signals the vanishing of the solid objectivity of the world. As the bonds with the outside world, within which paradoxically his love quest is confined, are severed, the mind turns on itself, fixes itself on its own elusive, chimerical figurations, and forgets its *aretè*, or virtue. It is at this juncture that, just as happens in the Senecan tragedies, in *Orlando Furioso* too madness takes over.

The scene of Orlando's madness occurs in canto XXIII, which is the numerical centre of the poem. Orlando, who had been pursuing Angelica, reaches a meadow and seeks repose in the cool shade of a grove. As always, in the epic, the experience of rest turns out to be the time of greatest danger. Repose is a trap whereby the unsuspecting, disarmed, at-ease hero is overwhelmed by dangers insidiously lurking behind the calm, pastoral surface of the surroundings.

In a nearby grotto and carved on the trunks of the trees shading the cove, Orlando reads that in this bucolic spot a simple shepherd, Medoro, loved Angelica. The text, written in Arabic, is decidedly Petrarchan: 'Liete piante, verdi erbe, limpide acque' (Cheerful plants, green grass, limpid waters) (XXIII, 108). It is as if Petrarch's lyric as well as the cosmopolitan Renaissance fashion of Petrarchism were understood by Ariosto to be the delirious crystallization of love discourse. Orlando reads the love poem, and his reading is a hermeneutics of the love conventions, the narcissism and evasiveness flanking them. The moods of his reading are artfully figured. At first Orlando archly dismisses the lines. They must be the erotic wishful thinking of some wanton boy. Subsequently (and narcissistically) he thinks they are written by Angelica only to tease him seductively and make him jealous. But his wishful thinking is soon over as it dawns on him that they tell a story from which he is painfully excluded. He grasps the message in the lines and goes crazy.

In a way, Angelica's choice of Medoro as a lover reflects her disavowal of the heroic ethos, and we shall see the implications of this later. For now, let me stress how the power of the story he reads shatters Orlando's mind. The grief the paladin feels is at one with the consciousness that Angelica is not his nor will she ever be. The recognition of his exclusion from her bliss moves him into a dim light that makes manifest to him, and to us, the limits of the powers of the self.

The vital centre of Neoplatonic thought, indeed its most substantial commonplace, lies in the assertion of the worth and nobility of man, who can ponder the plan of and wonder at the vastness of creation.[5] This doctrine, epitomized by Pico's *Oration on the Dignity of*

Man, finds its extension in this statement by Vincenzo Cartari, which I quote in the sixteenth-century translation of R. Linche: 'Onely man, whose body is framed erect, with his eyes still looking at that perspicuous and thought-amazing composition of the heavens ...' is invested with the gift of looking up.[6] Orlando's madness reverses this Neoplatonic tenet. Ariosto writes:

Fu allora per uscir del sentimento,
sì tutto in preda del dolor si lassa.
Credete a chi n'ha fatto esperimento,
che questo è 'l duol che tutti gli altri passa.
Caduto gli era sopra il petto il mento,
la fronte priva di baldanza e bassa;
né poté aver (che 'l duol l'occupò tanto)
alle querele voce, o umore al pianto.

L'impetuosa doglia entro rimase ... (XXIII, 112–13)

[He seemed at last as if about to swoon,
So nearly was he vanquished by his grief.
Do not dismiss the truth of this too soon:
I speak here from experience, in brief.
Of all the sorrows which the pallid moon
Surveys, this sorrow offers no relief.
He stands dejected, brow and chin held low,
His grief obstructs his words, no tears can flow.

The impetuous grief remained within ...].

The adjective 'impetuosa' is certainly to be taken in its technical sense from *epithumia*, desire; which is one of the four basic passions or impulses (the others, as I said earlier, are *phobos* [fear], *hedone* [pleasure] and *lupe* [pain]). Very simply, the adjective roots the madness of Orlando in desire. Furthermore, by the image of the head dropping to the chest (and later, the vacant gaze, the tearing of clothes, and other similar ones), the principle of Platonic rationality, of man's clear-minded reflective consciousness, is inexorably breached. In his madness the hero tramples upon all values as if they were hollow fictions: Nothing can define or confine him and, like a Machiavellian tragic figure, he can do what he likes. Orlando's madness, in effect, is tantamount to an unlimited, absolute power, and from this viewpoint it is the obverse side of the Renaissance myth – and of the Machiavellian prince – of boundless self-assertion. Ironically, in his madness, which effaces all simulations and accoutrements, the hero is no longer himself: He is literally alienated from himself and, paradoxically, now that he is without any disguises, he is most unlike himself, while the world is reduced to a phantasmagoria of the mind.

Ariosto's representation of madness departs from that of Seneca and of Erasmus (who edited Seneca for the Renaissance) in two significant ways. The first is that both Seneca and Erasmus uphold and dramatize what can be called the *discourse* of madness. In *Encomium Moriae* Folly speaks directly and, while she draws everything within her own ever-shifting horizon, her speech suggests the intelligibility of all reversals of sense that she operates. By the same token, because of his deep-rooted Stoic belief in the sovereignty of the logos, Seneca does not see madness as being outside of language or as marking the limits of language. His plays, not surprisingly, were not represented in the Middle Ages precisely because it was believed that they were meant to be spoken, in the assumption that their drama lies in the language and is at one with it. To the rationality of the Stoics madness appears as another discourse, the experience of unreason breaking through the convention of language but still audible to reason. But for Ariosto, as Orlando's voice obstructed by grief suggests, madness has no voice. It lies outside of language, and it can only be retrieved by the imagination, as Astolfo's retrieval of Orlando's wit on the moon makes clear.[7]

Further, and this is the second difference between Ariosto and Seneca, whereas for Seneca madness can be avoided by practising imperviousness to the passions, for Ariosto madness encircles the economy of passions, is undistinguishable from them, and is their epitome. Madness, as a matter of fact, is not only Orlando's sole prerogative, for all heroes of *Orlando Furioso* are involved in a form of delirium – in the etymological sense that they stray away from the furrow, the *lira*, and wander off the paths of Neoplatonic reason. In a way, Ariosto is here closer to the vision of his contemporary, Erasmus. Erasmus's Folly, as has been hinted earlier, camouflages herself in an infinite variety of masks, from court fools to pedants, from philosophers to warmongers to Christians:

> The Christian religion has a kind of kinship with folly in some form, though it has none at all with wisdom ... The biggest fools of all appear to be those who have once been wholly possessed by zeal for Christian piety. They squander their possessions, ignore insults, submit to being cheated, make no distinction between friends and enemies, shun pleasure, sustain themselves on fasting, vigils, tears, toil, and humiliations ... What else can that be but madness?[8]

Erasmus's Folly is the critical, even playful perspective from which he is enabled to satirize outdated beliefs, calcified opinions, presumptions of truth, dead metaphors, and empty propositions. As Folly attacks, most rationally and playfully, the predicament of rational knowledge, she appears as the creative, religious force unveiling the truth of the Pauline statement that the wisdom of this world is foolishness with God.

Ariosto is certainly close to this insight into madness by Erasmus. But he also differs from Erasmus in that he acknowledges madness to be not simply a serio-comical question of exposing how crazy the conventions of the social world are and how intellectually unfounded the determinations of rational sense. For Ariosto, on the contrary, madness is not merely an intellectual game that turns around all meanings; rather, it entails mind, desire, and body. More than that, the madness of Orlando in canto XXIII is punctuated by the words for grief – *dolor, duol, doglia* – that occur with obvious insistence (four times) in the space of nine lines. This grief, which is the attribute of Orlando's madness, marks the tragic disfiguration of the hero, his degradation into the sufferings of unaccommodated existence. Seen as an economy of suffering, madness for Ariosto is to be found in the war raging in the outside world of history; in the self-absorption of the mind; in the fascination with an idolatry of power, which invests the world with a substantiality it does not otherwise possess.

But does Ariosto envision any alternatives either to the tragic Machiavellian *Realpolitik* or to the Petrarchan mad lover? If the Stoic ideal of retreat from the world turns out to be illusory because, among other things, it denies the sovereignty of the passions; if the Erasmian wit is too complacently intellectual a game and ends up in moral indecision, what then, if anything, can and does Ariosto propose to counter the sinister dissemination of power as madness? The answer, very simply, is the world of play as it is incarnated by the poetic imagination, because play and art embody the mentality that both radically opposes and contains (in every sense of the word) the principles and practices of power.[9]

To be sure, the principle of play is characterized by deeply ambivalent values. On the one hand, play is linked to the utopian imagination and to the innocence of the child world: Spontaneity, innocence, and delight are, in fact, the main traits of the play experience. On the other hand, to play entails pretence, make-believe, and, as such, play recalls the various practices of simulation and artifice, which are overtly Machiavellian strategies of power. Much like Shakespeare in *A Midsummer Night's Dream* or Cervantes in *Don Quixote*, Ariosto gauges these troubling ambivalences at the heart of play. Agonic competitive duels among heroes; aleatory adventures; fortuitous encounters among characters; mimetic love rivalries or simulations of passions among lovers (see, for instance, the story of Olimpia); illusory exchanges of magic make-believe for reality (the witches Alcina and Logistilla); war games and jousts – all these are the variety of illusory forms that are the very stuff pervading Ariosto's narrative.

Ariosto inherits this sense of the play of illusory and deluding appearances, which variously mask violence or come through as sheer power-play, from both Ovid and Boccaccio. But Ariosto is also responding to Castiglione's sense of games as an aesthetic education. Whereas for Castiglione – and in this he is close to Machiavelli – aesthetics is linked to politics, in the sense that it is a way of constructing and controlling both the stability (forever vanishing) of one's world and the appearance of the self, for Ariosto play is a more encompassing category.[10]

The *Orlando Furioso*, for instance, is the playful reenactment of past literatures; it pokes fun at its own deluded claims and at those made by literature to freeze the flow of time and life itself; it invites us to laugh at the rich array of human fables; it asserts, as Astolfo's flight on the hippogryph exemplifies, the freedom of the aesthetic imagination. In short, for Ariosto play is nothing less than an *optics*, a certain manner of looking at the world. The world is certainly the theatre of power schemes and power fantasies, but to play means to occupy the standpoint that allows for the joyous assertion of the world of surfaces, of the fragments of contingency and time.

That time is the central concern of *Orlando Furioso* is made manifest by the snake of time – time as a snake biting its own tail – which is an emblem of the poem and which suggests time as the inescapable, eternal, self-generating circle of becoming out of its own ruins and ashes. It is made even clearer in the lunar cantos XXXIV and XXXV by the allegory of Father Time and of the Fates as bearers, respectively, of oblivion and death, against which the poem in vain wrestles; finally, the fragmentary narrative structure of the poem plunges us into a world of simultaneous temporalities where contradictory and disjointed actions quite coincidentally overlap. Time, I would suggest, is the real player in the poem; it is the invisible magician within the poem, forever playing with us and forever in flight, and forever capable of bringing about changes in the face of things, while the poetic imagination is the faculty that provisionally captures the shiftiness and insubstantiality of the world of time.

This overarching sense of the radical contingency of time and of the illusoriness of existence does not lead Ariosto to the conventionally sceptical position of the ironist who perceives the relativity of time-bound values. Such a posture is ultimately the ground for the moral justification or equivalence of all acts, because they are seen as lacking any intrinsic worth. And Ariosto, on the face of it, seems to fall within this camp, for – let me stress it once again – he constantly dramatizes both his consciousness of a ceaseless mutability within the horizon of history and the existence of alternate and limited visions of the real. From this standpoint he is a relativist who is aware of radically different and contingent world-views. But pure relativism is a problematic, if not false, notion, and in logical terms it is an outright impossibility.

Relativism, in fact, can be envisioned only on one paradoxical condition. Paradoxically, the relativist must posit that one's own relative, particular worldview can be transcended and a general standpoint can be attained so that other subjective views can be circumscribed, acknowledged, and made intelligible to one's own perspective. Ariosto's sense of the contingency of life thus presupposes the vantage point of an absolute experience. The narrative structure of *Orlando Furioso* lucidly enacts the logical paradox here described: The narrator is simultaneously inside and outside the story, and this means that Ariosto is supremely aware that the poet must step outside of his own worldview in order to represent different views. This double perspective is the constitutive trait of the play of the poetic imagination, whereby the poet confronts and is enmeshed by the ambiguities of all values but transcends them.

In the fictional world of *Orlando Furioso* nothing is ever absolutely true or untrue, which is another way of saying that everything is at once both true and untrue. The universe of simulation, fraud, games, and chance is the sinew of the poem, and it inexorably enacts forms of power. One might say that the poet, too, with his prerogative of including or excluding Machiavelli or whom he pleases from his fiction, and with his dependence on make-believe, shares in the general economy of power play. These power games, in which both characters and poet are involved, are primarily imaginative efforts to shape and control the world. Yet they also recognize that all the common acts of delusion and self-delusion depend on the assumption that reality is a play of appearances to be manipulated by the imagination. How are these two contradictory aspects of the text – the games of simulation and the disinterested play of the imagination – related to each other? And how, precisely, should the imagination be understood?

The poetic imagination is sovereign, and this sovereignty cannot' be reduced to a mere strategy of rhetorical simulations. The poetic imagination is akin to madness, yet paradoxically it retrenches from madness: It is a Platonic 'divine frenzy,' which possesses the poet and allows him to play with the world as madness (as is the case of *Don Quixote*, *King Lear*, and *Furioso*). Although it is radically unlike madness which, in Ariosto's terms, is the outer limit of language, it destroys nature, and is the negation of the work of art. More specifically, the imagination of *Orlando Furioso* contains a grammar of games (from those of chance to those of competition), a massive pattern of deluding artifices, and a visionary aspect of play. This can be called an ethics of play (as is also work), which the poetic imagination embodies, and this ethics is exemplified by a famous passage in Plato's *Laws* (803-4):

> Though human affairs are not worthy of great seriousness it is yet necessary to be serious; happiness is another thing. I say that a man must be serious with the serious, and not the other way about. God alone is worthy of supreme seriousness, but man is made God's plaything and that is the best part of him. Therefore every man and every woman should live life accordingly, and play the noblest game, and be of another mind from what they are at present. For they deem war a serious thing, though in war there is neither play nor culture worthy the name, which are the things we deem most serious.
>
> Hence all must live in peace as well as they possibly can. What, then, is the right way of living? Life must be lived as play, playing certain games, making sacrifices, singing and dancing, and then a man may be able to propitiate the gods, and defend himself against his enemies, and win the contest.

Plato's noble passage identifies play with peace and rejects war, which is the radical consequence of a power-based vision. So does Ariosto. Most canonical texts of the Renaissance explicitly reflect on play in its moral and metaphysical essence: from *The Courtier* to *Utopia* to *The Praise of Folly* (where madness is a form of play), from Tasso's *Gerusalemme Liberata* (where play is sacred) to Cusa's *De ludo globi* (in which reality appears as a cosmic game), and even to Valla's *On Pleasure* (which in its Christian Epicureanism presents life as a feast to be enjoyed) – they all focus on play as the state of freedom of the mind. *Orlando Furioso* plays a pivotal role in this great conversation of the Renaissance as it steadily shuttles between, on the one hand, play as competition and simulation and, on the other, play in the ethical significance of peace assigned to it by Plato.

Ariosto's poem contains simultaneously all of these ideas of play – make-believe, competition, fiction, illusion, the reader's comic amusement, the magic manipulation of appearances, madness as the principle of disorder (akin to the carnivalesque play), music, and aesthetic pleasure. It also dramatizes a vision of harmony and peace. To be sure, the epic genre is always rooted in war, but the question of peace figures prominently in *Orlando Furioso*. As a matter of fact, in the most 'Machiavellian' section of the poem (cantos IX and X), Ariosto features Cimosco, who is a Machiavellian 'fox' and 'lion.' Cimosco, who is a king forever given to deception, has the mythical status of the first man to introduce firearms in wars. Orlando's ultimately futile yet arresting gesture is to throw the cannon into the bottom of the sea.[11]

The hero's gesture may strike the reader as Ariosto's ironic nostalgia for a heroic time when war had, as it were, a human face – when duels were fought, and through the duels justice was being done; it may even be a hint of Orlando's own self-delusion, for his action is not the rejection of the heroic *ethos* that he as a paladin incarnates; most certainly it will not stop the textually imminent violence at the siege of Paris. In effect, the riddance of the cannon suggests, more than anything else, the paladin's aesthetic horror of infernal war machines. Yet it is exactly as an aesthetic act that the gesture had radical implications for Ariosto's playful and ethical vision.

By the time Ariosto wrote and rewrote *Orlando Furioso*, he knew that he had to be a poet, and he must also have known that probably there was no other choice for him. What he must have persuaded himself about, one guesses, is that the language of poetry – and not, say, Aristotelian rationality, which here appears highly precarious, and even less discursive and literal texts on the desirability of peace – is the paradigm of ethics. Poetry is the model of ethics, because it is marked by disinterestedness and the pleasure one links with play. Above all, it is the model of ethics in the sense that it is inherently constituted by contradictions: Its material sweetness is a powerful medium of seduction, yet the knowledge it provides is unreliable; its rhetorical strategies can be overt or hidden, yet it becomes a vehicle for noble ideas. These contradictions do not cancel each other but always implicate each other and are the core of the poetic text.

All of this amounts to saying that Ariosto's poetry is the art of an ironic double vision, or to put it somewhat differently, aesthetics necessarily counters the values of war: Whereas war makes the admittedly partisan and partial interests of one side absolute, the play of the imagination, such as Ariosto's, thrives on ambivalences and resists raising the partial half-truths claimed by one side to the level of the truth. Machiavelli, consistently with his ideas of power, writes the *Discourse on the Art of the War*, to which readers of the Renaissance can oppose Erasmus's *Querela Pacis* (The Complaint of Peace). Ariosto makes poetry, which in its ambivalences and irreducibility to a single literal viewpoint always recognizes the discourse and viewpoint of the other, the absolute model of ethics and harmony.

Readers of *Orlando Furioso* have been right in suggesting that art is the transcendent and absolute aim of this poem. I certainly agree with this traditional formula for the epic, but I would like to suggest that poetry for Ariosto is not a self-enclosed construct; rather, it involves itself in faculties such as ethics and politics and it is rooted at the centre of the most radical questions debated by the Renaissance – power, war, madness, the passions, and peace. Ariosto's vision, in short, acknowledges the contradictory impulses in our perception of the real and points to the centrality of poetry for restoring sanity to the hero.

What invests poetry with such value is the fact that poetry playfully shares even in the values it denies. In this ambivalent and constitutive playfulness poetic metaphor discovers and evokes the vital unity linking the contradictory and problematic heterogeneity of all phenomena – war and peace, madness and love, the passions, and so on. More to the point, in *Orlando Furioso*, the metaphoric unity of its heterogeneous fragments is made quickly evident by the musical harmony, itself traditionally the result of discordant strains, which Ariosto's *ottava d'oro* in its melodious fluidity manages to recreate. It is also made evident by the poetic flight of Astolfo, which invites us, in turn, to move back and forth, as if in the precarious balance of a dance, across disparate boundaries of experience.

As the poet's imagination soars, it summons us to let our imagination run loose and yet be mindful of Astolfo, be mindful to retrieve, like Astolfo, one's rationality and return to the world. Like Prospero in *The Tempest*, the poet discovers, in short, the necessity of bringing one's own visions and art back to reality. It may well be Ariosto's ironic, subtle playfulness at the end of the poem that has him show the poet getting a glimpse of the shore and yet remaining at large. Had he got closer, he probably would have seen Machiavelli in the cheering crowd.

3. Adventures of Utopia: Campanella, Bacon, and The Tempest

In Chapter XV of *Il Principe*, Machiavelli summarily dismisses the utopian tradition of political philosophy. Utopian fantasies, such as the Renaissance figurations of the 'città felice' (Alberti, Leonardo, Filarete, Patrizi, and others), serve no useful purposes. The same holds for classical schemes of moral philosophy – such as those that were articulated in the feigned commonwealths of Plato and Thomas More (whose *Utopia*, published in Louvain in 1516, was debated by the Italian humanists). They are so abstract and remote from the real ways of the world that they are more likely to cause ruin than self-preservation:

> Ma sendo l'intento mio scrivere cose utile a chi la intende, mi è parso più conveniente andare drieto alla verità effettuale della cosa, che alla imaginazione di essa. E molti si sono imaginati repubbliche e principati che non si sono mai visti né conosciuti essere in vero; perché egli è tanto discosto da come si vive a come si doverrebbe vivere, che colui che lascia quello che si fa per quello che si doverrebbe fare impara piuttosto la ruina che la perservazione sua: ... Lasciando, adunque, indrieto le cose circa uno principe imaginate, e discorrendo quelle che sono vere, dico che ...

> [But since my intention is to write something useful for anyone who understands it, it seemed more suitable to me to search after the effectual truth of the matter rather than its imagined one. And many writers have imagined for themselves republics and principalities that have never been seen or known to exist in reality. For there is such a gap between how one lives and how one ought to live that anyone who abandons what is done for what ought to be done learns his ruin rather than his preservation ... Leaving aside, therefore, the imagined things concerning a prince, and taking into account those that are true, I say that ...][1]

I have referred to this passage in the previous chapter. I shall stress here that what matters for Machiavelli is the concrete data of empirical experience, the reality of facts that can be known and understood. Not that appearances or facts are transparent or coincide with their hidden sense. The phrase, 'a chi la intende,' gives the hint of a surreptitious message, of a covert, even esoteric lesson hidden in the folds of Machiavelli's explicit discourse on power. It suggests that in *The Prince* there are apparent meanings for the many and truths reserved for the rare and the few. We are admonished to be alert to a hermeneutics of a double discourse. In effect, the phrase hints at a politics of ambiguity: It conjures up a hierarchy of intelligences, an intellectual elite capable of deciphering the secret enigmas of power or *arcana potestatis*. From this aristocratic perspective, utopias are dangerous and fantastic imaginings told for the benefit of the many. They are dangerous because they betray – so Machiavelli implies – reality itself or the way things really are. They are dangerous and delusional dreams because they make impossible, false promises of non-existent perfection, which, in turn, is based on the seductively false notion of the perfectibility of human beings. In this sense, utopian discourses foment illusions about who we are by forcing on us abstract images of who we ought to be.

In reality, then, Plato's and More's utopias are deceptions. In reality, we are simultaneously half-men and half-beasts, as the secret, ancient teachings of the centaur Chiron to Achilles – necessarily kept hidden from the many – exemplify (*The Prince*, chapter XVIII):

> Pertanto, a uno principe è necessario sapere bene usare la bestia e
> l'uomo. Questa parte è suta insegnata a' principi copertamente dagli
> antichi scrittori; li quali scrivono come Achille e molti altri di quelli
> principi antichi furono dati a nutrire a Chirone centauro, che sotto
> la sua disciplina li custodissi. Il che non vuole dire altro, avere per

precettore uno mezzo bestia e mezzo uomo, se non che bisogna a uno principe sapere usare l'una e l'altra natura; e l'una sanza l'altra non è durabile.

[Therefore, a prince must know how to use wisely the natures of the beast and the man. This policy was taught to princes allegorically by the ancient writers, who described how Achilles and many other ancient princes were given to Chiron the centaur to be raised and taught under his discipline. This can only mean that, having a half-beast and half-man as a teacher, a prince must know how to employ the nature of the one and the other: and the one without the other cannot endure.] (pp. 133–4)

Secrets about how to use the beast and the man, how to undertake bold action, and how not to observe faith lie at the heart of Machiavelli's conceptual enterprise. They give intellectual coherence to   his anti-utopian political discourse. Utopias – as visions of the self-over-coming of human beings, and of the philosophers' dream of freeing humanity from history – would be possible 'if men were all good' (p. 134). But they are a bad lot. It follows that, in order for the prince to overcome, he must free himself from current standards of good and evil. He must mask his desires; and, paradoxically, he must make a tendentious spectacle of his most fearsome and secret actions.

This theatre of power – made of simulations and dissimulations, rhetorical or carnivalesque masks and tricks – is crystallized by Machiavelli's *Mandragola*. The same reduction of reality to the empire of simulacra and to a play of appearances, the same reduction of politics to an occult and circumspect science or magic imposture is prominent in *The Prince*. Chapter XVIII of this text continues by evoking Pope Alexander VI, who 'did nothing else ... thought about nothing else, except to deceive men' (p. 134). The chapter concludes by reversing Ficino's Neoplatonic universe of metaphysical essences. Over and against Ficino's theory of the essential reality lying behind the cover of illusory phenomena, the world of fictions and appearances – for all their falseness – is for Machiavelli a positive doctrine and the paradigm of realism:

> A uno principe, adunque, non è necessario avere in fatto tutte le soprascritte qualità, ma è bene necessario parere di averle. Anzi ardirò di dire questo, che, avendole e osservandole sempre, sono dannose; e parendo di averle, sono utili; come parere pietoso, fedele, umano, intero, religioso, ed essere; ma stare in modo edificato con l'animo, che, bisognando non essere, tu possa e sappi mutare el contrario.

> [Therefore, it is not necessary for a prince to have all of the above-mentioned qualities, but it is very necessary for him to appear to have them. Furthermore, I will be so bold as to assert this: that practicing them at all times is harmful; and appearing to have them is useful; for instance, to seem merciful, faithful, humane, forthright, religious, and [perhaps even] to be so; but his mind should be disposed in such a way that should it become necessary not to be so, he will be able and know how to change to the contrary]. (pp. 134–5)

From these strategies whereby appearances are equated to nothing, and whereby one possibly fulfils one's designs, it follows that politics is logically envisioned as an economy of power. Its pursuit implies the necessity of a secret and conspiratorial art. Because one cannot trust appearances or public postures and discourses – they are the realm of tricks and make-believe – one can only trust oneself. The practice of *dissimulazione onesta*, as Torquato Accetto was to call it later in the seventeenth century, marks an Epicurean ethics. It is an ethics of retreat into the inviolable interiority of oneself, into a philosophical garden, away from the turmoil and deceptions of history. There is also a theological equivalence to this philosophical sense of the pure interiority of the self: It is the Augustinian or Lutheran idea that the essence of the self lies in one's own innermost interiority.

From Machiavelli's own point of view, the focus on politics as occult magic inaugurates the emergence of Renaissance scepticism or doubt about the real. The primary locus where scepticism emerges is the philology of Lorenzo Valla, which exercises a methodical doubt about the 'true' meaning and authenticity of texts. Its origin goes back to the Roman rhetorical-legal traditions of debating the 'evidence.' Machiavelli's philosophical scepticism is to be understood as limiting the knowledge of the external world or the triumph of private forms of knowledge over and above public discourse. This sceptical epistemology sustains the practice of power: It is the power to confer a sense on the ceaseless, random, and inexplicable play of events; it is the power to bring to reality the figments of one's own imagination.

Many objections were raised against Machiavelli's realistic, de-idealized political theories. They were denounced too by the tradition of the 'anti-Machiavel' (Botero, Gentillet, Lipsius, Ribadeneira, and others).[2] These anti-Machiavellians are, with a few exceptions, religious thinkers. They are Jesuits, who hold fast to their beliefs that morality and politics need not be thought of as irreducibly antagonistic to each other. Tommaso Campanella's *Atheismus triumphatus*, in which Machiavellianism is connected with the libertinism of the Epicureans, who believe in nothing, reflects the anti-Machiavel. No doubt, the principles and theories of the anti-Machiavellians are bound to appear suspect. There is nothing more Machiavellian than a thorough profession of anti-Machiavellianism. Sustained objections to Machiavelli's dismissal of utopias are launched by both Campanella and Bacon. In *The City of the Sun* and the *New Atlantis* they both begin by retrieving the very utopian discourse Machiavelli rejects as unworkable fiction.

For Machiavelli, classical utopias are not compatible with the immoderate passions of the modern age. They preach restraint as a moral virtue and consider the excesses of individual freedom a vice. By contrast, in the modern world of Ficino's and Pico's Neoplatonism, man's power and freedom have no formal limits. In the boundless freedom of the self – so holds Pico in his *Oration on the Dignity of Man* – lies man's distinctiveness. Within the scope of the new, gigantic ambition to conquer nature and fortune, Aristotelian moderation is not a virtue. The new political science Machiavelli provides must deal with the realities of the modern project and seeks to supersede the limitations of the ancient discourse. That he is aware that fortune exceeds the reach of virtue only adds heroic pathos to man's likely defeat.

The *New Atlantis or Bensalem* rewrites Plato's fable of Atlantis destroyed by an earthquake, as one reads in the *Critias*. *The City of the Sun*, in turn, is an essentially Pythagorean utopia, the geometric-arithmetic graph of political harmony. In this musical economy, the jarring tension between quality and quantity is discreetly masked. Quite overtly, however, the title eclectically alludes to Ficino's Neoplatonic-Orphic *De sole*; to Dante's Heaven of the Sun (*Paradiso*, X–XIII), which is the planet of arithmetic and the house of wisdom; and to Isaiah's prophecy of 'the city of the Sun' (Is. 19:18).

From Campanella's and Bacon's viewpoints, Machiavelli's realistic reduction of politics to a sinister economy of power had misunderstood the political need for utopias and utopian thinking. Utopias are necessary for many reasons. One reason is that there is always a need to accommodate the excess of private desires to the public good, politics to ethics, moderation to freedom. This is the overt project both Campanella and Bacon pursue in their fictions. At the same time, even as they argue for utopia, they both perceive the limitations of ancient utopianism. The perfect regime envisioned by classical utopian thought – from Plato to More – seeks to fill the gap between moral philosophy and political philosophy. Their utopian vision of moderation and order, however, is the crystallization of an underlying contemplative vision.

As Machiavelli knew, utopias are unrealistic, vain flights of the imagination. So, just as Campanella and Bacon criticize Machiavelli's realism, they also update and revise Plato's contempt for the practical or productive arts. Accordingly, they offer a serious modification of Plato's belief in the merely fictional existence of utopia. The new sciences of the modern age – of which both Campanella and Bacon are philosophers – can demonstrably make a new world and effectively build Plato's best regime. It follows that human rationality can conquer nature; man's need for justice, order and peace – which contemporary religious warfare and Machiavellian politics had obliterated – can truly be established.

From this standpoint of a feasible reality (which Machiavelli had called for in the final chapter of *The Prince*, devoted to the making of a new Italian state), both *The City of the Sun* and the *New Atlantis* espouse the innovations of the modern scientific project. In addition to Neoplatonic and Dantesque echoes, the 'city of the sun' recalls Augustine's *City of God* as well as the new heliocentric astronomy dominating sixteenth-century European debates. Copernicus's astronomical revolution was endorsed by Bruno in the *Ash-Wednesday Supper* – a dialogue that takes place in London, at the house of Fulke Greville (who, for a time, was Bacon's friend). It was endorsed by Kepler's *Harmonice mundi* and Galileo's experimental science.

The primary intent of both Campanella and Bacon is to show the alliance of politics and science. In *The City of the Sun*, Galileo's telescope is the emblematic technological device by which modern science redrafts the architecture of the heavens. With Campanella, thus, we are in the sunlight of a scientific and metaphysical order, and its political refractions. By the same token, the *New Atlantis* opens a doorway into the future: Bensalem, which in Hebrew means 'off-

spring of peace,' is a 'model' or the 'College of the Six Days' Works.'
Its aim is to enlarge 'the bounds of human empire to the effecting of all
things possible.'[3] By the triumph of medicine and the 'Divine Pool of
Healing,' diseases are cured, lives prolonged, bodies preserved, experiments of light performed, and natural catastrophes – such as earth-
quakes, thunderbolts, and floods – are contained. In this utopia of
science – where the 'spy-glass' is a most recent technical innovation – a
new Genesis or a new creation is at hand. Divine knowledge is within
man's reach and making.

If Bacon's word, 'model,' implies the articulation or reduction of
knowledge to a mechanical, orderly program, the discovery of Bensalem, as much as the discovery of the 'city of the Sun,' depends on
chance. The implied link between science and chance demands a
gloss. The *City of the Sun* is constructed as a 'poetic dialogue,' in the
mode of Platonic and Renaissance dialogues. The interlocutors are a
knight of Malta (of the order of St John in Jerusalem) and a 'Gen-
ovese' who was one of Columbus's sailors. The text, thus, comes
into being in the wake of the real voyages of discovery of the New
World.

The Genoese had sailed around the world and had reached Tapo-
brana. There he was forced to put ashore and hide in order to escape
the fury of the natives. By the same token, *New Atlantis*, which
W. Rawley calls a 'fable' in order to suggest its fictional, unreal (not
yet existent and yet feasible) status, begins with the account of a ship
that sails from Peru until 'it comes to pass' that the sailors find
themselves without food in the midst of the uncharted wilderness of
water. In the universe of science, as in the world of the Machiavellian prince, chance or fortune is the prerequisite of virtue. Science
aims at the conquest of error and of the voluble wheels of chance. It
is the route whereby the 'occasions' of Fortune and fortuitous occur-
rences are drawn into the mechanical regularity of the pattern.

Furthermore, the two texts show that to reach the plain of science, one must traverse the chancy, risky 'wilderness' of the sea. The sea, which in traditional iconography is the seat of shifty Fortune, stands for the enigmatic, unpredictable, and dangerous scenario of nature. Odysseus, the hero of the Neoplatonists, travels to strange lands in search of wisdom over forever vanishing sea lanes: The sea is unconquerable and affords no pre-established routes of knowledge. In the age of Columbus and Drake, the sea is the very emblem of Bacon's thought. Bacon, who is a sort of Drake, compares himself to Columbus (*Novum Organum* I, 92). The comparison is predicated on their common virtue in conquering vicissitudes and making bold advances toward truth. Accordingly, the frontispiece to the *Great Instauration* features a ship going beyond the Pillars of Hercules. In the emblem, navigation puts to the test man's power over nature.

For a new universe to move into view, knowledge must turn into a transgression. This was the way of Ulysses and Columbus. The philosophical resonance of the scientific discoveries of the modern age suggests that, for both Campanella and Bacon, modern science is the daylight of the ancient sages' dream. It also suggests that, for both of them, science, more than an end in itself, purports to be the risky, uncertain path leading to philosophical wisdom. Yet, the promise is that science will conquer chance. Machiavelli's doubts about virtue conquering fortune are now superseded.

That this is the thrust of *The City of the Sun* is suggested by its subtitle, 'poetic dialogue.' 'Poetic' – as one evinces from Campanella's own *Poetics* (1596) – connotes a knowledge that is also a 'making,' or a productive activity. A 'dialogue,' on the other hand, describes a philosophical genre *par excellence*. It designates the text as philosophical theatre, and casts it as literally a utopian dialogue between poetry and philosophy, making and knowing. Nonetheless, Campanella's dialogue in no way recalls a dialectical disputation, of the type one finds in medieval debates or in the dialogical form of Platonic and Renaissance philosophy. These traditional structures are marked by an oppositional rhetoric that expresses itself through irony; it aims at bending the interlocutor's will and at resolving all contradictions.

Campanella articulates his text within the horizon of Plato's dialogues. There is not in it, however, the elenctic or logical refutation nor is there a unification of antithetical viewpoints. Rather, the knight of Malta questions the Genoese and, in the process, the dialogue turns into an adventurous quest of discovery. Nor is there a conclusion to the exchange: The Genoese constantly comes and goes, is always on his way, somewhere else, and at the end he interrupts himself. Pressed by the Knight of Malta to discuss how the Solarians understand the religious divisions of modern Europe or the religious colonization of Mexico by Fernando Cortés, the Genoese replies: 'Non posso, non posso' (I cannot, I cannot).

The open-endedness of the text, in point of fact, discloses Campanella's sense of the modern impossibility of what the humanists had practised and dubbed 'civile conversazione.' If from a formal perspective the dialogue implies the truly utopian possibility of thinking otherwise, of opening oneself to the adventure of a possible discovery of an unpredictable viewpoint, of a perspective different from ours, the Genoese sailor's interruption draws attention to the riskiness of speech, to the necessity of taking cover or being evasive or deploying a double-speech. Thus, utopian, solar knowledge is shrouded by steady enigmas. Or, to put it differently, there is a gap between the transparent solarity of utopian discourses and the murkiness or danger of the unsayable in the world of history.

This gap ostensibly highlights the uniqueness of the city on the hill, which, like the sun in the Copernican universe, is situated at the centre of the world. More to the point, the city of the Solarians came into being as a philosophical community:

Questa è gente che arrivò dalle Indie ed erano molti filosofi che fuggirono le rovine di Mogari e d'altri predoni e tiranni; onde si risol-

sero di vivere alla filosofica in commune, si bene la communità delle
donne non si usa tra le genti della provinzia loro, ma essi l'usano, ed
è questo il modo. Tutte cose son communi; ma stan in man di offi-
ziali le dispense, onde non solo il vitto, ma le scienze e onori e spassi
sono in communi, ma in maniera che non si può appropriare cosa
alcuna.

[This is a people that came from India, many of them being philosophers, who fled before the depredations of the Tartars, and other
plunderers and tyrants, and they resolved to live in a philosophic
community. Though community of wives was not practiced in the
land they came from, they do practice it now, and in this manner: all
things are held in common, but the dispensation of goods is left in
the hands of officials. Not food alone, but arts, honors, and pleasure
are also shared in common in such a way that no one can appropriate
anything.] (pp. 36–9)[4]

The Machiavellian world of tyrants, predators, and individualism
is superseded by the city of philosophy and its *libertas philosophandi*.
As befits a city of philosophers, it is not a city of mere needs. Mere
needs degrade humans into beasts. On the other hand, desires,
honours and pleasures – experiences that are individualized and,
therefore, divisive – inexorably encourage destructive rivalries. In
Campanella's text, these passions are simultaneously acknowledged
and effaced by an impulse to realize the principle of general sharing.
Against this background, Campanella's philosophy comes through
as an attempted harmonization of all contradictions. More than
that, he articulates a Pythagorean theory of harmony in which the
views by Ptolemy, Copernicus, and Galileo are reconciled.

The topography of the city – circular in shape with seven concen-
tric circles bearing the names of the seven planets in the Ptolemaic
cosmology and with four gates at the four cardinal points – enacts

the geometric-mathematical principles of the Pythagorean architecture of the cosmos. In the *Republic* (401, 6–10), mathematics represents the purity of knowledge. In the *Metaphysics* (A5) the Pythagoreans are said to cultivate mathematics as if numbers were the principle of all things. *The Life of Pythagoras* by Jamblichus records ascetic life of containment and overcoming of the passions as well as common ownership of property as the two distinctive traits of the ancient Pythagorean communities in the south of Italy.

The City of the Sun retrieves all these traditions. It casts astronomy, mathematics, music, ethics, and the practised education of the Solarians in the Pythagorean musical/religious terms of the 'harmony of parts and whole' (p. 56). We are told that the Solarians believe, as the Pythagoreans do (cf. Ovid's *Metamorphoses* XV), in the kinship of all things. They live in the light of a Pythagorean ethics of moderation, wherein even sexuality is monitored. They uphold equality. The city is governed by the principle of universal education: All are taught the knowledge combined in one book, 'in the manner of the Pythagoreans.' The point is that the Solarians are constituted as a Pythagorean, scientifically minded community of scholars in pursuit of encyclopedic knowledge. The chief discipline is astronomy, but the curriculum of the *trivium* and *quadrivium* is crowned by Metaphysics.

In spite of the egalitarianism shaping the political economy and public consciousness of the city, the structure of the government is hierarchical: A Metaphysician, who has the sense of the whole, and who rules because he has the sense of the whole, hovers over the three princes (Power, Love, and Wisdom). All together, they have set up a panopticon by which they control the city's goings-on. Spies abound in it; all secrets are forbidden except for the secrets of the state and the secret self-sufficient existence of the city itself. In effect, Machiavelli's conspiratorial vision is surreptitiously restored in the political practice of utopia.

The perfect city of Plato's *Republic*, available only in speech, is envisioned as ruled by the philosopher-king. Plato posits philosophy as the royal road to truth and, at the same time, he makes politics the sovereign end of philosophy. Like Plato and More, Campanella insures the dominance of philosophy, as if it were the way out of the madness of sectarian beliefs ravaging Europe. Like his two pre-modern predecessors, he takes the path of philosophical wisdom and makes science its handmaiden. In the light of this new hierarchy of philosophy over sciences, Campanella's idea of absolute, transcendent knowledge that translates into absolute power is not just a dystopic element in the narrative.

The union of knowledge and power in *The City of the Sun* is an explicit response to the challenges of both the new experimental sciences and Machiavelli's new political science. In an apparent and real endorsement of Galileo's new map of space, Campanella will write a few years later an *Apologia pro Galileo*. The *Apologia* is also a critique of Galileo. The *Sidereal Messenger* had demolished the illusions of a hierarchical universe and the attendant complacent geometric myths. Galileo's heliocentrism had boldly retrieved a Pythagorean doctrine, which for Campanella is a way of saying that wisdom is the mother of science. The endorsement of the scientific project hides a critique. For all its brilliance, the modern scientific discovery has silenced the 'harmony of the spheres' and has produced no ethics of harmony. *The City of the Sun* has filled the gap science could not fill.

In point of fact, Campanella aligns Galileo with Machiavelli, and he comes to grips with the necessary modern alliance between the magic of politics and the truth of science. Galileo's telescope unveils the real structure of the cosmos and shows phenomenal appearances – the apparent immobility of the earth – to be illusory. In the name of science, Galileo eschews deceptions and does not 'save appearances.' Machiavelli sifts reality from mere imaginings. In the persuasion that images are the displacement of reality, he sceptically focuses on the manipulation of all appearances. Politically, the scepticism of the one is as dangerous as the realism of the other. Machiavelli's non-utopianism is dangerously naive to the extent that it misses the necessity of utopias or the necessity of the noble lie, which science promises to realize. The opposite is also true: The secret machinations of power are necessary to preserve the ideal Pythagorean order of the city.

The weave of Pythagoras's harmonics, Galileo's scientific truth, and Machiavelli's mystique of power lies behind Bacon's utopia of science in the *New Atlantis*. But Bacon goes beyond Campanella's philosophical project. In the scientific and secretive society of the New Atlantis, science is wisdom. The Bensalemites have knowledge of all the sciences, arts, and inventions. They have power over wind and sea. And they intend to re-make Divine Creation: Scientific discourse is for them an updated Edenic language, wherein words and things coincide, and lies are obliterated. More specifically, Bacon presents his utopian 'fable' (a term that entails both speech and fiction) as a Machiavellian strategy of power and as a mode of preserving the empire of science. Science is the source of power, and it must be sheltered from impostures.

Much as the *City of the Sun*, the Baconian world is governed by secrecy. The laws on secrecy, promulgated by Solamona, hold sway: The existence of the island is kept hidden from strangers and likely intruders. Travel out of the island is restricted; tight surveillance on all aspects of life is observed; eugenics is enforced; spies are sent out to gather scientific information. The scientists take an 'oath of secrecy,' conceal experiments and inventions from the State, and have developed techniques of magic illusion. Above all, the practice of religion is permitted only by the judgment and decision of the scientific elite: The people of Renfusa (etymologically, 'sheep-like') are allowed to accept Christianity by one of the 'wise men of the society of Solamon's House' (p. 48). In an open acknowledgement of their superior status, the scientists of the 'College of Six Day's Works' are given generous rewards. Statues are erected to them, while their servants live frugally. Science, then, subdues nature and is the foundation of power, including the power to establish values.

There is another crucial difference between *The City of the Sun* and the *New Atlantis*. The final section of *The City of the Sun* turns into a prophecy of a new dawn of history and a new aesthetics. The chief sign of the new age is the expanding Spanish empire, which was heralded by Columbus and through which the world is to be united under one law. In the *Monarchy of the Messiah*, Campanella invests the Spanish crown with messianic, soteriological attributes. In *The City of the Sun*, however, Spanish universalism and discoveries of new lands are hampered by Spain's 'hunger for gold.'

Even so, the new beginnings of history are adumbrated by the signs of the times: Galileo's discovery of the 'canocchiale' or looking-glass; the invention of the 'oricchiale' (so-called out of symmetry with 'canocchiale'), a phantasmic device by which to hear the music of the spheres; and the imminent discovery of the art of flying. The new age is announced by the advent of women rulers all over Europe: Bona in Poland; Mary in Hungary; Elizabeth in England; Catherine in France; Mary in Scotland; Isabel in Spain. This new age of women-rulers is heralded, so Campanella claims, by Ariosto, 'the poet of this century,' who sings of 'Ladies and knights, of arms, of loves' (p. 123).

The telescope, which is the mechanical prolongation of Alberti's 'perspective,' is a fixed, individualized contraction of the classical 'vision of the world.' It marks the reduction of essences to pure phenomenality, as if what appears to the privileged viewpoint of the scientists truly is. The 'oricchiale' and music, on the other hand, free us from the rigidity of the fixed, mechanical viewpoint. The musical aesthetics of Ariosto's epic – acknowledged by Galileo, by Bruno in his *Cena delle Ceneri* (Dialogue II), as well as by musicologists such as Giandomenico da Nola, Cipriano da Rore, and Giovanni Bardi – embodies the harmony of the new age.

In doing this, Campanella may have intuited the anti-Machiavellian polemic artfully woven in the folds of *Orlando Furioso*. At any rate, *The City of the Sun* tells, like *Orlando Furioso*, an epic adventure. Ariosto's epic, simultaneously solar and lunar, with its discontinuities, multiple plots, disintegration of Neoplatonic rationality, and transcendent vision counters for Campanella the theocratic colonization of Mexico by Fernando Cortés, who establishes Christianity in Mexico. On this remark, as we recall, Campanella prudently interrupts the 'dialogue.' As the Genoese says 'non posso, non posso,' the text reaches the limit of discourse: It reaches the point where discourse has no place. In this sense, Campanella's 'poetic dialogue' is the utopia of a man who dreams of a world in which philosophy and poetry, sun and earth, madness and reason find their *concordia discors* or Ariostan harmony. Thus understood, the text is the utopia of a man who, from the depths of the Neapolitan jail in which he writes, lives his solar, shadowy solitude.

The *New Atlantis* gives Campanella's prophetic vision an enigmatic and specifically political twist. This text, too, is unfinished, and we have to ask ourselves why. One reason is Bacon's belief that science alone is equipped to construct and give a definitive shape to utopia. Not to finish the text is also to intimate that his vision is only realized by the process of 'making,' by the translation of the 'fable' into 'fact.' There is another reason for the text's incompletion. In the *Advancement of Learning*, which unfolds a new intellectual order for the conquest of nature, politics is called, in Machiavellian terms, a 'secret and retired art.' It is secret because its knowledge, as if it were a hermetic, magic cabala, is too dangerous to be shared. What is it that Bacon cannot openly share?

The *New Atlantis* is the secret blueprint or 'model' (as if it were a mechanical mold) for the political order that the *Advancement of Learning* had promised but, apparently, not delivered. Just as the *Advancement of Learning* aims at countering the traditional control of learning by the church, the *New Atlantis* promises to replace the (Catholic) Spanish empire with a new British empire. It is as if Bacon, like Columbus of old, promises King James I how Great Britain can lead the world to the scientific hegemony and rationality of Bensalem. Accordingly, the consciousness of the Spanish empire and the Spanish language punctuates the text. The sailors who visit Bansalem come from Peru. They speak Spanish. They learn how the ceremonial Christianity of Renfusa is subordinate to the civil religion of the merchants of light. The victory over the Spanish empire and its excesses (pointed out by Campanella) takes place by envisioning a world community ruled by science. Bacon's own English text marks the beginning in the process of circumvention of the empire of the Spanish language.

One text deliberately seeks to escape the logic of power inscribed in both Machiavellian practices and Platonic utopias. Shakespeare's *The Tempest* provides a critical perspective on the utopian fables of both Campanella and Bacon. It begins by openly evoking the Machiavellian world of conspiracies, simulations, and seditions that both Campanella and Bacon had craftily hidden and Bacon had practised in his own text. The political background of this 'Italian' story (the historical alliance between Milan and Naples to offset the hegemony of Florence) gives the play its intellectual density. Prospero is an encyclopedist. He spends his time in the pursuit of the 'liberal arts' and 'secret studies' (I, ii, 73, 77), which are not Machiavelli's *arcana potestatis*. Nor is there in Milan room for the philosopher-king. Prospero's brother, Antonio, carries out a coup d'état and usurps power. The liberal arts, clearly, cannot save one from tyranny.

Defeated, Prospero turns to magic or secret knowledge to exorcise the dangers of new intrigues and the conspiratorial machinations of his servants. In his island, which is a playland of the imagination, he enjoys limitless freedom and sovereignty over a reality he has created through the power of his imagination and the deployment of new illusions and dissimulations. He becomes a truly Renaissance *magus*, like Bruno, or a rhetorician who understands the magic power of conjuring up the phantoms of the mind and making people believe in things that do not exist. He sets up a magic new world, wherein all that is imaginable is possible.

In the utopia he builds, Prospero follows the Neoplatonic doctrines about hierarchy and value that both Ficino and Pico had advanced. Ficino's and Bruno's speculations about occult secrets of hermetic magic are tied to Pico's vision of man as a work of indeterminate form and the most fortunate of creatures. He is worthy of admiration, says Pico in his *Oration on the Dignity of Man*, because he is free and unconstrained by any limits. He is capable of moulding himself at will and choosing his essence. Magic, the art of making illusions out of nothing, crystallizes Pico's theories. He asks: 'Who does not wonder at this chameleon we are?'

The question encapsulates Pico's sense of the grandeur of the human mind, its power to make new worlds. It also betrays his intellectual imperialism, wherein he casts himself as the lord of all esoteric knowledge – a view that was highly influential in England as soon as Gianfrancesco Pico published his uncle's *Opera omnia* in 1496. (Thomas More, as is known, translated into English Pico's *Life* by Gianfrancesco.)

The political magic of *The Tempest*, as much as Machiavelli's, Campanella's, and Bacon's, has its foundation in Pico's philosophy of knowledge as making. What Pico saw as the power of the intellect to grasp the secrets of creation, wend one's way among the stars, and trespass the boundaries of the natural world, Prospero translates into political/intellectual power. His exercise of power encompasses the theatre's illusions, music, rhetoric, and the power of the imagination. In the process, he conjures up both a Machiavellian world – in which the magician/rhetorician rules over the 'mechanical arts' of Caliban and the 'liberal arts' of Ariel – and an alternate vision to the world of Milan and Naples.

The complicity between metaphysics and politics shapes Ficino's relation to Cosimo de' Medici in Florence. Prospero knows that one is the truth or mirror-reflection of the other. The rigidly hierarchical lines, along which political life on the island is organized, reflects the complexity of his understanding. Aesthetics is subordinated to the political exigencies of stability and power. At the same time, the metaphysical centre of Prospero's symbolic cosmos resides in Pico's view of man. When in wonder Miranda beholds Ferdinand, she voices Pico's perception: 'I might call him / A thing divine; for nothing so natural / I ever saw so noble' (I, ii, 418–19). Miranda herself, by a transparent pun on her name, appears to the lost and confused Ferdinand to be a 'wonder.' The word restates Pico della Mirandola's sense of wonder as the origin of knowledge. Prospero is the hidden cause of wonders.

As the agent of the wonders, Prospero's art is the art of the maker. He knows he is not a self-sufficient maker: He needs the mechanical labour of Caliban and the art of execution of Ariel, who is the free spirit of music and for whom the island is too narrow a prison. In truly Piconian fashion, they all want freedom and resist Prospero's authoritarianism. They go against the limited awareness he had as duke of Milan: In Milan, his pursuit of the liberal arts was an end in itself. On the island, he understands that he has to co-opt poetry, music, theatre, and the lowly arts for his rule. Although *The Tempest*, on the face of it, treads the road blazed by Campanella and Bacon, it does not limit itself to harmonizing Plato and Machiavelli, or science, magic, and politics.

By the end of the play, Prospero abandons his secret and magic arts. We are usually told that Prospero's withdrawal from the stage of power reflects his wisdom about time, finitude, and the limits of power over nature. I would like to add that the Epilogue spoken by Prospero discloses Shakespeare's extraordinary insight into world-making or life as theatre. In what way is 'theatre' the very metaphor of cosmopoiesis or world-making?

To view the world as if it were only the world we make carries with it the exhilaration of imaginative freedom from the constraints of nature and history. The primacy the Renaissance gives to *vita activa* tells us we are free to the extent that we invent ourselves. Nothing matters, so it is said, if not what we can make. We are chameleons, have no pre-established essences, and we are, thus, better than angels. Angels occupy a fixed place in the chain of being. Human beings have no fixed essences and are, therefore, freer than angels. The world that matters is the world we bring into existence, like magicians, out of nothing.

Pico, Machiavelli, Campanella, and Bacon saw in this exhilaration the trace of man's artful divinity or, at most, Prometheus's proud transgression of the power of the gods. Shakespeare sees more. He sees unreality lying at the heart of making and as the outcome of making. If we are chameleons who become all we touch, then, we may really be nothing of our own.

As he connects making, freedom, and magic, making is the mask of non-being or nothing. In a way, Prospero gives a retrospective self-justification of the time he spent engaged in secret studies and contemplative studies before the conspiracy against him took place. In and of itself, contemplation may mean an inept disengagement from the exigencies of time and active life. Nonetheless, active life, which ostensibly is a turning of the gaze toward the real business of the world, in and of itself ends up in the pursuit of nothing: Nothing exists before one makes it. Prospero's farewell to his art is a farewell to a making that dissolves, melts 'spirits into air, into thin air.' As the play is played out, he lets us see the pursuit of nothing as the essence of the fascination the modern world holds for making. Over and against Pico and Bacon, Prospero understands that to conquer 'nothing' one has to submit to it. Contemplation, which celebrates the carving of sacred time out of the nothingness of fallen time, is the way out of nothing. Obliquely, he summons us to rediscover the necessary interdependence of *vita activa* and *vita contemplativa*.

4. The Ludic Perspective: Don Quixote *and the Italian Renaissance*

In part II, chapter XLI of *Don Quixote* there is a memorable and pivotal shift in the narrative. After trying to stave off what to him appears to be a potentially dangerous adventure, Sancho mounts Clavileño, the wooden toy horse sent by the sorcerer Malambruno to the Duke and Duchess. Clavileño was originally Merlin's contraption, and its magic powers make it akin to other horses – so Sancho is told – from classical Greek myth to the Italian Renaissance epics. The text punctiliously enumerates their names: Pegasus, the winged horse of Poetry; Bucephalus, Alexander's horse; Orlando's Brigliadoro; Rinaldo's Bayard; and Ruggiero's Frontino, to mention only some of them. Sancho's fear is overcome. Riding on Clavileño's back, Don Quixote and Sancho will undertake a flight to the kingdom of Candaya in order to achieve what no cosmetics can deliver – to restore the natural appearance of the women's faces disfigured by Malambruno's enchantment.

Let me begin by musing on a central feature of Cervantes's style that occurs in this passage – the enumeration, or epic catalogue. The catalogue of horses, which will go on to include Rocinante and the Palladium, the wooden horse left by the Greeks on the plain of Troy, aims at encompassing the whole classical and Renaissance tradition. As a trope of enumeration, the catalogue constitutes what I call a 'perspectivistic space' – an archaeological site wherein Cervantes oversees the whole of literary history up to the present, inscribes himself in it, and wills to move beyond it.

In strictly thematic terms, Sancho's adventure on Clavileño marks a decisive turn in the economy of the novel toward a specifically political focus. Chapters XLII and XLIII, as a matter of fact, feature Don Quixote's advice to Sancho before he goes to govern his isle. In chapters XLIV and XLV Sancho takes possession of the isle, and we are given a fairly detailed account of his government. The overtly political narrative is interlaced with digressions about Don Quixote's battle with persistent phantoms and other temptations to his chastity.

What is the link between the squire's political experience as governor and the visionary flight on the back of Clavileño? Are vision and politics discontinuous from each other, and in what way does political theatre depend on some other vision, as I argue it does? And what does this relationship mean for Cervantes's sense of a tradition that he encompasses and wills to transcend? To put it differently, what exactly is Cervantes's understanding of the *arcana potestatis*, the magic and enigma of power, that steadily reveals itself as sorcery? But, first of all, what happens to Sancho on his flight? Let me go back to chapter XLI.

Sancho's adventure on Clavileño is unequivocally announced as a trick or a hoax, a *burla*, contrived by the Duke and the Duchess for their pastime. It is a playful and even innocuous diversion feeding on an overt artifice and an array of false elements: fake beards, cosmetics, non-existent sorcery, caricatures, and deformation of reality. For his part, Don Quixote, who is a dupe to his phantasms and clings to the notion that no clear line can be drawn between knowledge and belief, quickly agrees to undertake the new chivalric adventure that La Dolorida or 'the afflicted woman' demands of them. Tricks, after all, are never completely false; and if they are false, they are diabolical modes of revelations to be exorcised by his noble art, or ways in which the (shifty) magic appearances of the world are commonly perceived.

But the flight on the back of Clavileño is memorable and pivotal in the economy of the narrative for what happens to Sancho. He has so far remained aware of the true and the false, of the difference between acts and reveries in the master's conduct. Whereas the knight is not blinded by the light of the obvious but only by the dazzlement of beauty, Sancho relentlessly practises double vision. He is torn between the awareness of the true and the false. Now, however, for all (and because of) his fear of heights and distance from the earth, as he imag-

ines he is galloping Clavileño, Sancho's mind approximates the visionary state that marks the normal condition of the knight.¹

Blindfolded, both Sancho and Don Quixote imagine their voyage
through a Ptolemaic space – the three-tiered cosmos of earth, air,
and fire. The flight begins as bystanders warn the would-be-questers
not to re-enact the hubris of a famous mythological occurrence:
'Tente, valeroso Sancho, que te bamboleas! Mira no cayas; que serà
peor tu caída que la del atrevido mozo que quiso regir el carro del
Sol, su padre!' (p. 332) (Hold on, valorous Sancho, you are swaying.
Be careful not to tumble. For your fall would be worse than the rash
youth's who sought to drive the chariot of his father the sun)
(p. 730). The allusion recalls the myth of Phaeton who drives the
chariot of the sun and falls down. Stylistically, the allusion to the
myth is a transparently hyperbolic counter to Clavileño's own flight.
For the myth of Phaeton (much like the myth of Icarus) tells the
story of overweening pride, of the 'rash youth' who wants to overcome and transcend the father and to occupy a higher place than the
father. The possibility concerns Cervantes's own relation to and
place in the tradition. More poignantly, by a subtle stroke, Cervantes stages the metaphoric cluster of pride/ hyperbole/ and perspective. Pride – like hyperbole, which is disproportionate language
– is shown to be a question of perspective: It signals the awareness,
such as Lucifer's, both of what is above oneself, that is, of gaining
God's own standpoint, and of the danger in abdicating the distance
between oneself and what is above oneself.

If there is a danger that the knight and his squire may be like Phaeton or Icarus, the danger may be true, as hinted earlier, for Cervantes himself and his perspective on the whole tradition. For now,
however, the flight is seen as revelatory of an absolute, visionary
standpoint. The knight knows the implications of this adventure:
'No repares en eso, Sancho; que como estas cosas y estas volaterías

van fuera de los cursos ordinarios, de mil leguas verás y oirás lo que quisieres' (pp. 332–3) (Pay no attention to that, Sancho. For as these matters of flight are out of the ordinary cause of things, you will see and hear what you please a thousand miles away) (p. 731). Thus, he bids Sancho not to open his eyes, and, in effect, he makes physical blindness the condition for vision. Sancho, however, undaunted by the warning that his curiosity may be a trick of the devil, wants to know the limits of his adventure.

He cheats and he peeks at the earth from under his handkerchief covering his eyes:

Yo, señora, sentí que íbamos, según mi señor me dijo, volando por la región del fuego, y quise descubrirme un poco los ojos; pero mi amo, a quien pedí licencia para descubrirme, no lo consintió; mas yo, que tengo no sé qué briznas de curioso y de desear saber lo que se me estorba y impide, bonitamente y sin que nadie lo viese, por junto a las narices aparté tanto cuanto el pañizuelo que me tapaba los ojos, y por allí miré hacia la tierra, y parecióme que toda ella no era mayor que un grano de mostaza, y los hombres que andaban sobre ella, poco mayores que avellanas, porque se vea cuán altos debíamos de ir entonces. (p. 335)

[I felt, lady, that we were going, as my master said, flying through the region of fire, and I wanted to uncover my eyes a bit. But when I asked my master's leave to take off the bandage he wouldn't allow me. But as I have some spots of curiosity in me, and want to know what is forbidden and denied me, softly and stealthily I pushed the handkerchief that covered my eyes just a little bit up on my nose and looked down towards the earth. And the whole of it looked to me no bigger than a grain of mustard seed, and the men walking on it little bigger than hazel-nuts. So you can see how high we must have been then.] (p. 733)

At this point the knight and the squire are made quickly to tumble to the ground. Like two puppeteers, the Duke and Duchess pull them down in an overt vengeful desire to humiliate them or, as it were, bring them down to earth. But the fall does not humble them. So committed is Sancho to the vision he has experienced that nothing can really drag him down. In this radical shift in perspective, the fall gives him, paradoxically, what can be called a spirit of gravity.

What Sancho says he sees actually flattens all differences between the great and the small on earth: Everything amounts to nothing, or to Lilliputian proportions. The diminutiveness of the human that his stance discloses makes him provisionally lose interest in the prospective government of the island. There is a touch of pride in Sancho's indifference. Pride ontologically reveals the presence of something superior to oneself (we always feel pride in the presence of what we perceive as higher than we are). Morally pride is objectionable because it entails contempt or disinterest for those one perceives as below oneself.

Sancho's flight and vision recall a number of traditional visionary flights: from Plato to Cicero (where vision is a condition for politics), from Dante to Chaucer, from Boccaccio to Astolfo's flight on the hippogryph. But there is a particular text that stands behind Sancho's description and which is of the greatest importance to the Renaissance comical discourse, Lucian's *Icaromenippus or the Sky Man*. The text is a dialogue telling the ascent of a philosopher who transgresses the limits of ordinary perception and who, from the ironic standpoint of a transcendent vision, laughs at the spectacle of human life. Menippus, it can be said, is the Cartesian philosopher as spectator, and his laughter is the mark of his fall. Appropriately, he is compared to Icarus whose flight, like Phaeton's, ends in disaster:

I was especially inclined to laugh at the people who quarrelled about boundary lines ... As a matter of fact, as the whole of Greece as it looked to me then, from on high, was no bigger than four fingers, on that scale surely Attica was infinitesimal. I thought, therefore, how little there was for our friends the rich to be proud of. It seemed to me that the widest-acred of them all had not a single Epicurean atom under cultivation. And when I looked toward the Peleponnesus and caught sight of Cynuris, I noted about a tiny region, no bigger in any way than an Egyptian bean, had caused so many Argive ... to fall ... I laughed heartily ... for the whole of Pangeum, mines and all, was the size of a grain of millet.

FRIEND: But the cities and the men ... how did they look from on high?

MENIPPUS: I suppose that you have often seen swarms of ants ... The cities with their population resembled nothing so much as ant-hills.[2]

Lucian's laughter is the epitome of the ironic *serio ludere*. Playful and earnest laughter entails the ironic style, and it makes Lucian the classical point of reference for the likes of Alberti, Erasmus, Thomas More, Montaigne, and Ariosto himself. Lucian's irony is the rhetoric of a hierarchical vision – a hierarchy of knowledge, time, and value – and of the reversibility of perspectives. In such an ironic stance they all saw the basis for a perspectival view of knowledge, which is to be understood as a knowledge that shifts according to place and time. This type of historical knowledge is at the heart of modern debates and the style of modernity. Cervantes, much like Ariosto, fully grasps the implications of the Renaissance perspective. Like Ariosto, he makes it the object of his critique.

The question of perspective (which in the Middle Ages was variously theorized by Alhozen [965–1036], the Silesian Witelo, and by Roger Bacon) belongs to the science of optics, and concerns itself with the nature of light, colour, and the anatomy of the eye as preconditions of vision. But by 1600 *perspectiva*, which is understood as *perspectiva artificialis*, defines the illusory geometry of a pyramidal perception. Its principles were put into practice by the architect Brunelleschi, but its chief codifier was Leon Battista Alberti. In his treatise *On Painting* (1435), Alberti makes of painting the art of Narcissus, and of perspective the aesthetics of geometry.

In pre-Renaissance painting, objects are depicted independently of one another, as they are known to be. By contrast, the mathematical law of perspective simulates distance and represents objects not as they are, but as they appear to be according to one's place in the field of vision. 'Vision,' Alberti writes, 'makes a triangle … and from this it is clear that a very distant quantity seems no larger than a point.'[3] Playing on the etymology of *history*, from the Greek *historeo* ('I see'), Alberti says that a painting tells a *historia* describing how the parts of a thing fit together. Perspective, then, is the artifice of composing and fitting disparate things together. Yet, for all its irony, there is a touch of Lucianesque laughter in Alberti. The story of Narcissus, who for Alberti is the inventor of painting, hints that by perspective the eye sees only itself and that perspective is an optical illusion, a play of appearances which derealizes the world and transforms it into an empty appearance.

It falls outside the focus of this discussion to show, for instance, how Pulci's *Morgante*, which is the playful story of a voracious giant, who seems to be on the verge of swallowing up the world and of seeking to reduce it to nothing, dramatizes the myth of the Renaissance and the myth of the overman as the meeting point of the trope of hyperbole and perspectival science. And I will only suggest that the Cartesian spectator who wants to look at truth in perfect clarity – Erasmus, More, as well as Ariosto and Cervantes, with their rhetoric of ironic reversibility of perspectives – translates Alberti's science of perspective into a question of spatial style.

Leo Spitzer recognized long ago that perspectivism defines the dominant mode of Cervantes's writing.[4] The Prologue to *Don Quixote* dramatizes the stylistic eclecticism of the novel, the will to connect into a *synopticon* and a *historia* the different partial styles of tradition. More importantly, Sancho's voyage on Clavileño, as the squire claims to have reached the transcendent viewpoint from which he sees the world as a whole, turns into what I take to be Cervantes's real concern: exposing the limitation of Renaissance perspective as a way of knowing; recovering a 'world-vision.'

Let me recall the two major antithetical reactions to Sancho's visionary claim. One is by the Duchess; the other is by Don Quixote. The Duchess sees the world from her perspective of political power and sense. She knows that there is a sharp and real division between a toy and a horse, the make-believe of play and truth, and she tries to convince Sancho that he really saw nothing. In what is a transparent rehashing of arguments drawn from Renaissance debates on perspective, she remarks to Sancho that what he saw – the earth like a grain of mustard, and man like a hazel nut – is out of proportion and that 'we do not see the whole of what we look at from one little corner' (p. 734). From her point of view, in effect, Sancho takes the part for the whole. Because he forgets this, he is deceived by his experience.

Don Quixote, on the other hand, at first sceptically discards Sancho's visionary claims as a 'dream or a lie.' His reaction is strange. Earlier he had believed that giants had turned into windmills. Further, by a deft and unequivocal Cartesian twist, he claims: 'I think and so it is true.' His scepticism may be his way of testing Sancho's visionary claims as 'a dream or a lie.' But the knight's scepticism also suggests his possible belief that a true vision is accessible only to him, that only he has the superior perspective on the nature of things. He concludes, thus, that Sancho has lapsed into either self-deception or a deliberate misrepresentation and falsification of the real occurrence. Because it is usually the knight who changes images into essences, and because Sancho is usually prey to an empirical mythology, the charge that he is either dreaming or lying is Don

Quixote's way of linking the playful diversion of the Duchess, the world of play, dreams, and lies as all part of an imaginary experience. They are hints that the boundary line between truth and falsehood is a faint trace.

There is a strange power and a magic trickiness to play and dreams in that they reveal the inconsistency of the real. From this standpoint, hoaxes, lies, and dreams are the key to the possible vanishing of the way the world is perceived. The issue, however, is not simply that one imagines what one sees, nor is it about the necessity of imagining the world. As the knight dismisses Sancho's account as a dream or a lie, he points to what he perceives as Sancho's real blindness, the impossibility of his seeing what he says he sees. The point is that Don Quixote, whose life is commonly described as ascetic, in effect, puts forth the insight of mystical discourse, with its 'madness' and its dazzling blindness.

That Cervantes is here engaged in a sustained reflection about the depth and ambivalences of the imaginary world in its wide spectrum – from the mystification of everyday banality to the illusion of Countess Trifaldi, to the make-believe of the Duke, and to the phantasmagoria of the knight and squire – is evident from Don Quixote's final remark to Sancho: 'Sancho, if you want me to believe what you saw in the sky, I wish you to accept my account of what I saw in the Cave of Montesinos. I say no more' (p. 735). The statement unites two modes of vision and calls Sancho – as well as us – back to the knight's project. What did Don Quixote see in the cave of Montesinos? How do the two scenes explain each other?

Let me quickly look at the story of the cave and its dramatic context. In what turns out to be a play to show the practical, contingent value of tricks, Basilio has tricked all the spectators at Camacho's wedding (Las bodas de Camacho) (II, XXI). Don Quixote emerges from the crisis as a 'Cid in arms and a Cicero in eloquence.' Seized by a great desire 'to see with his own eyes' and test the truth of the marvellous stories he has read, he asks for a guide to lead him to the cave.

The guide, who is himself versed in reading books of chivalry, and who calls himself a 'humanist,' has already authored *The Book of Liveries*, which is a description of devices, mottoes, and ciphers. The textual detail casts the guide as an emblematist and it evokes Alciati's and the baroque world of emblems and *picturae*. For all his laughable pedantry, the humanist works at the perpetual and obscure boundary where enigmas and images converge, where signs and occult ciphers, language and vision intertwine. Like the knight, the guide reads books of chivalry. And like the knight, 'who wants to see with his own eyes,' the guide is a Baconian empiricist. He tests the claims and authority of tradition and is engaged in a lateral quest for observable knowledge. He has already produced a book on the *Spanish Ovid* that, one imagines, retrieves the allegories of errant shapes in Ovid's *Metamorphoses*.

The guide's likely visionariness translates itself now into an empirical science of order and encyclopedic totality. In his sublime naivety – wherein the sublime is to be taken as the trope of elevation and/or the opposite of irony – he is preparing what he calls a *Supplement to Polydore Vergil*. The supplement is to treat of the 'Invention of Things.' The humanist defines it as a work of great erudition and research into 'matters of great importance omitted by Polydore.'

No doubt, the humanist quests for a knowledge which, by reasonable standards, is not worth knowing or possible to know. He wants to know who the first man in the world was to have catarrh, and who was first to use ointments to cure himself of the French pox. The humanist's science is archaeology, a science of historical origins and foundations that, ironically, lie outside any empirical realm. Sancho dismisses the guide's whole project by referring to Lucifer and to Adam as the first tumblers of history. Sancho's joke drives home an important point: An empirical history of knowledge ends up in a myth of origins, for all origins and foundations are obscure and unknowable. But there is another and serious side to Sancho's joke. There is in the joke an oblique link to what he will find out later in his flight on and tumbling from Clavileño: The hyperbolic dream for a total knowledge is the obverse side of the fall; more than that, Sancho conveys the comical understanding of the necessity to take the comical perspective of the fall.

Above and beyond the dynamics binding together the characters, the reference to Polydore Vergil affords Cervantes the point of confrontation with and the standpoint to interpret the practical assumptions of Italian humanism. To make my argument clear, let me begin with a question. Who was Polydore Vergil?[5] An Italian priest and humanist who lived in England. While in London, he enjoyed the friendship and, eventually, was a correspondent of Erasmus, More, and Colet. His *Inventions of Things* (Venice, 1499) is a veritable archaeology of knowledge or a 'heurematography' – a research into the origins of man's téchne and practical arts. A counterpart to this encyclopedia – which is in part patterned on Isidore's *Etymologies* – is his *English History*. As a work of political history *Historia Anglica* casts politics as a practical art. It also reveals how a quest into inaccessible distant origins turns into a modern political project, into a project for feasible new beginnings. Polydore Vergil does not finish his *History*. The text comes to a prudently evasive end with the story of Mary, the daughter of Henry VIII, and Catherine of Aragon.

Cervantes may or may not have known Polydore Vergil's *Historia*, which possibly was the point of departure for the Jesuit political theorist Pedro de Ribadeneira's *Memoir on the Conversion of England* of 1596. At any rate, the knight is an archaeologist like Polydore and like the humanist. At the same time, Cervantes himself, in his perspectival writing, seems to take on the role that the guide takes toward Polydore. He supplements what the Renaissance epic had left out. But the knight is also unlike the guide or Polydore: Whereas the encyclopedists seek to rationalize the myth of origins, the knight re-mythologizes knowledge.

The humanist's quest, for all its absurdity, is the necessary preamble to what turns out to be the knight's descent into the cave of Montesinos, which amounts to a descent to the very ground of his being. Yet, by his descent the knight radically re-orients the humanist's random, lateral quest for fictional beginnings. And with the knight's descent Cervantes re-orients literature itself beyond the profound ironies of Pulci and Boiardo. The cave of Montesinos is the knight's archaeological site, the subterranean realm of frozen memories and dormant fictions. In this obscure region, which turns out to be a palimpsest of literary dreams and of the wonders of the Arthurian and Carolingian cycles, the knight falls asleep. As he wakes up he sees a castle of transparent crystal and Montesinos himself, who shows Don Quixote the sepulchre where Durandarte is kept enchanted by the wizard Merlin.

The knight's experience marks a sudden separation in the sense of *historia* and it introduces two distinct orders of historical knowledge. *Historia* is not just a fabric of natural observations, as the humanist believes. It is also, like Alberti's view of painting, a visionary text interwoven with legends, heraldry, chivalric memories, and archaic narratives. In this other history, Don Quixote reaches the truly utopian point where the past appears as death. As he digs into the burial ground of history and its sediments, his memory is the oracle telling him, through the sage Merlin, that he himself will revive the ancient cult of chivalry. He has, thus, learned that the value of mythic origins lies in their magic power to determine the plot of history and its future forms.

Historically, the knight's descent into the cave recalls Ulysses's *katabasis*; Aeneas's vision/dream through the gates of horn; the Platonic myth of the cave and of Er's descent to Hades; Dante's journey; and even the underworld of Boiardo's Morgana (*Orlando innamorato* II, viii). Like the knight's, these are journeys that bring the heroes 'home,' to a spiritual centre or to a place from which every soul starts out on its exile or errant journey. In this place Don Quixote 'sees with his own eyes and touches with his own hands,' and the phrase, which comes from the Acts of the Apostles, seals his experience beyond all possible doubts. Sancho takes his master's account to be a sign of raving madness (p. 623), and when asked if he thinks his master lies, he equivocates. For his part, the humanistic pedant extracts from the knight's vision impossible evidence for his chimerical project of a totalizing positive knowledge. The empiricism of one, however, is the obverse side of the other's scepticism.

Does Don Quixote know, or can we suspect, that he is lying? At the beginning of part II, chapter XXIV, in a marginal comment Cide Hamete notes his doubt about the literal truth of the adventure, 'for it exceeds all bounds of reason' (p. 624). He adds that the knight, who was a most truthful gentleman, would not tell a lie. At any rate, Cide Hamete goes on to say that Don Quixote on his death-bed retracts the story and confesses he invented it. He did so because it fit the chivalric tales he had read ('cuadraba bien con las aventuras que había leído en sus historias.') To put it differently, what is the relationship between Don Quixote's and Sancho's respective visionary claims?

Don Quixote, the reader of books, affirms the existence of a world he had found in his romance, 'en sus historias.' Books have the power, as do magical or cabalistic formulas, to cast a spell on him. Thus, he affirms literature's specific privilege and role in creating reality. And as in mystical experiences, his idea of literature is the unavoidably errant translation of an ecstatic vision, whose truth he wills to reconstitute. In this sense, Don Quixote does not lie, or he lies the way a mystic lies in translating vision into language: He believes what he says, even if the language unavoidably betrays the essence of the vision. By the same token, as the knight gauges Sancho's adventure on Clavileño in the light of his own vision in the cave, he sees Sancho discovering storytelling as a personally private, false and yet irrefutable perspective on the world. Whereas one brings all perspectives to a necessary absolute vision, the other makes vision a literary and counterfeit perspective.

In their distance from and complementarity to each other, the two visions of the knight and the squire stand for two different but mutually implicating ways of understanding literature. By their specular economy, each mode of understanding literature gives the lie to the other, and each is the truth of the other. To determine what these two literary modalities are, which are included in the wide compass of Cervantes's novel, we must look at the scene that follows Sancho's vision. The focus of the narrative shifts largely to politics, to the account of Sancho's finally becoming the governor of his island. By the narrative shift, Cervantes lucidly grasps, as the Italian humanists, rhetoricians, theorists of education, and Polydore Vergil had done, that in order to speak of politics one has to speak of literature first, that fiction is the crucial ingredient of political discourse.

The move from literature to politics is not without danger. Accordingly, Cervantes begins his representation of the movement from the global, transcendent vision on the back of Clavileño to the political world of partial and competing viewpoints by an ironic counter. We are told that, before the flight on Clavileño, the knight gets off the horse in order to find out what it hides in its interior. The toy horse could be a contraption like the Palladium, the Trojan horse within which Greek soldiers hid when Troy fell. By the detail, given *en passant* as part of a mock-heroic fantasy, he subtly tells us of the politically disruptive power of art: Ulysses's contrivance of the wooden horse is the means by which the Greeks enter and destroy Troy from within. He is also reminding us of what Plato states in the *Phaedrus*: Rhetoric is the art invented by Ulysses in the leisure hours of the Trojan war. Rhetoric, in short, edifies cities and also destroys them. By so doing, Cervantes introduces us to the knowledge that using fables as preambles to or as necessary fictions of political mythology presents a fundamental danger.

The danger with fables is that they make us imagine as being possible events which, by the realistic standards of reason, are not. They make us form extravagant, even irresistible projects beyond ordinary strength. Don Quixote's extraordinary vision – achieved by his going down below the ground – lifts man as close as possible to the divine perspective, whereby human beings can overcome all difficulties and impose their infinite will on the world. In short, he summons us to a noble task, without which life is like the flat expanse of his plains.

Don Quixote's vision of wonder – which is the beginning of all knowledge – is his way to rise and have us rise above the human, his way to bring death back to life. In this sense, he promises a boundless utopian knowledge, which is the privilege of God. But the promise ends up as a politically unfeasible stance, as an errant fiction in a world that stubbornly remains human and that must remain human in order to be lived in by humans.

On the other hand, there is Sancho's vision. Though self-induced and though distinguished by an initial contempt for and realization of human pettiness (which is the essence of pride), it reveals a truth: the truth of the prideful perspective of the first tumbler Lucifer. Sancho's vision is a lie or a fiction of the whole. As a lie, it partakes of tricks engineered against him by the Duchess, who thinks of herself as the hidden puppeteer of an amusing show. By lying, Sancho has become her accomplice. But as a fiction, it is the fiction of a theoretical totality which is revealed as the necessary foundation for the political project. Such a project can only be realized, not through the partial self-interest of the productive arts, but as the *composition* of the parts made to fit into a whole. To say it differently, pride is what

Sancho experiences in his ascent. Understood politically, pride entails always the question of one's place in the mobile scheme of things. It defines the human perspective that makes Adam or Lucifer want to be like God and to rule. It also reveals one's contempt for what is below oneself or for oneself seen as if one were below others. From this perspective, pride is both necessary for and destructive of the city.

Cervantes endorses the humanist's project of a totality as the science of the whole. As if to suggest the interdependence between the domains of knowledge and action, he has Sancho become the governor while Don Quixote plays the theoretical role of adviser to the Prince.

His point of departure is the need for Socratic self-knowledge and care of the self: 'procurando conocerte a ti mismo, que es el más difícil conocimiento que puede imaginarse' (You must keep in view that you are striving to know yourself, the most difficult thing to know that the mind can imagine) (II, 42, p. 738).[6] Why is it difficult to know oneself? Is it because we find this knowledge unbearable? More concretely: What does the Delphic oracle – know thyself – mean? It is a call to moderation. It also means that to know oneself one has to know the whole; that one knows the whole only if one knows oneself, or that one knows oneself only in the light of the whole. In terms of Plato's *Republic,* government is, first of all, a rule over the economy of the passions and the tyranny of immoderate *eros.* In effect, Don Quixote evokes for Sancho's benefit the classical project of the just city. Such a city is not the city of needs, which is the City of Pigs. Nor is it Kallipolis, which, being close to the gods, is unlivable for human beings. The just city, on the contrary, begins with the care of the body and of the mind, in the awareness that politics is both a question of the immoderate desires of the body and of proud minds eager for infinite knowledge.

Earlier Don Quixote had celebrated the pastoral utopia (I, XI) of the ascetic containment of bodies. That evocation worked as Cervantes's strategy for rejecting the modern political Machiavellian project of infinite desire, which he identifies through the figure of the 'Cretan labyrinth' (p. 86). In this place, sovereignty is accorded to the voracious man-beast (Machiavelli's Minotaur) and to Plato's *pleonaxia*, the tyrannical and unjust desire in the soul of the city. But there is an alternative to pastoral self-denial and Machiavellian desire, and it is somewhat different from Ariosto's.

Don Quixote's advice follows the model of the Christian humanists Erasmus and More, first of all, in the key realization that securing good counsel is crucial to good government. It follows also the substance of the *Christian Prince* by Pedro de Ribadeneira (1595), which is a refutation of Machiavelli. Ribadeneira bases his treatise on Erasmus's *Education of a Christian Prince* (written for the future Charles V at the same time as More's *Utopia* [1516]). Like Erasmus, Ribadeneira advises the curtailing of extravagances and luxuries at court; the cultivation of justice in one's soul; the art of peace; the emendation of laws; the danger of idleness; the tyranny of self-serving judgment. This wisdom stands behind Don Quixote's counsel and Sancho's practice. And there is a pointedly ironic detail in Cervantes's deliberately recalling the Erasmian model. Erasmus believes that the prince should be taught edifying literature. This is literature, in the manner of the tales of Aesop (p. 211), that has a clear ethical sense. If the clear sense is missing, it is the teacher's duty to bring it out. Literature is to be taught allegorically and as a moral means to a desirable end. Erasmus adds that the prince should be taught about Phaeton as the parable of a young man who wills to guide the chariot of the sun and takes the reins from his father Apollo. The fable shows the story of a prince who 'seized the reins of government and ... and brought ruin upon himself and the entire world' (p. 212). Consistent with his ironic vision – which transcends ironies – he holds that, because a boy by nature ferocious can easily become a tyrant, he should be provided with antidotes to the stories of Achilles or Alexander the Great. And he bluntly rejects as politically disruptive the fables of Arthur and Lancelot which are 'not only tyrannical but also ... foolish.'[7] Such a rejection of romances and fables parallels the ascetic rejection of the world by pastoral utopists as well as Sancho's rejection of politics. But where does Cervantes stand?

For all his irony, Cervantes, I submit, agrees with the Erasmian view of the relation between literature and politics. As we recall, at the point where the knight retrieves his sanity, he acknowledges chivalry as a dangerous enterprise and gives up its books. The act simply acknowledges what the novel has been telling us all along: Literature exceeds the bounds of reason and can disrupt its economy in the 'desocupado' (unoccupied) reader. But the political fable of Sancho's brief government brings to light the other effect fiction has on political power. Essentially, it shows that politics does not flow from Don Quixote's discourse of truth but from Sancho's self-assertive lies. Don Quixote's madness is his utopia, both in the sense that madness stages a utopian world where all exchanges are possible and in the sense that he is nowhere, forever out of place, choosing 'la discreta y desenvuelta' Altisidora. By contrast, Sancho diligently makes his rounds of the isle.

Pedro de Ribadeneira – like a host of other anti-Machiavellians such as Scribani and, eventually, Diego Saavedra Fajardo – asks if it is possible for a good man to rule or if the ruler is inevitably corrupt. Sancho, who has his understanding of the whole, shows that he can rule. But after a week of governing, he chooses to go home and take care of his garden. Politics is not a practical art for him, and utopia has contracted to the perimeter of one's own backyard. He leaves, unaware that he has been the butt of a joke, unaware that politics is the sceptical theatre of puppeteers, who are experts in the hidden games of power.

As Sancho leaves, Cervantes writes the emergence of the modern project. In such a project, political power is neither the productive art Sancho wants it to be, nor is it a contemplative art of the whole as Don Quixote knows it must be at its root. In his ironic vision, politics has become a technological art of occult powers. But there is Cervantes's own politics.

What remains truly political is Cervantes's novel itself as the reservoir of the language of a nation and of the Latin American imagination. In this sense, Cervantes's novel, which encompasses absolute vision and partial perspectives, traces an alternative future. Such a future needs both Ariosto's sense of madness and Don Quixote's madness in order to divine new departures for thinking. Of the two, Ariosto is the greater poet. But he looks backward and, thereby, he seals an epoch. Cervantes looks back, but only to retrieve Boccaccio's prose for his own novellistic experiments. With *Don Quixote de la Mancha*, with the work of art as prose, the modern age begins, and with it begins the novel of the future.

The age of prose contemplates the poetry of the Italian Renaissance epic – Pulci, Boiardo, Ariosto, and Tasso – as if it were a distant dream of Edenic wholeness. And as happened in Poliziano, Ariosto, Tasso, Bruno, Campanella, Bacon, Shakespeare, and Cervantes, this dream of the Italian Renaissance is the dream of the world: of world-making, actual worlds, possible worlds, golden worlds, brazen worlds, the creation of the world, and the metaphysics of infinite worlds.

This cosmopoiesis rests on and needs a prior vision of the world, a contemplation of the whole wherein the arts of making acquire a purpose beyond their limited purviews. On the necessarily shaky, dangerous foundation of the Renaissance world-vision and world-making, the modern world rethinks itself and experiments itself. Only by drawing from this imaginative and spiritual reservoir will there be once again a rebirth of myths and memories for the future.

Notes

1 POLIZIANO'S *ORFEO*

Much valuable work has been done on Poliziano's intellectual role in the Italian quattrocento. Here I limit myself to recording some key bibliographical items that shed light on my own reconstruction of Poliziano's poetry and thought. See E. Garin, 'Filologia e poesia in Poliziano,' *La rassegna della letteratura italiana* 58 (1954), 349–66; J-P. Barricelli, 'Revisiting the *Canti carnascialeschi*,' *Italian Quarterly* 43 (1967), 43–61; R. Bessi, 'L'area culturale della *Nencia da Barberino*,' *Interpres* 1 (1978), 59–95; S.B. Chandler, 'La figura poetica di Lorenzo de' Medici,' *Letterature moderne* 7 (1957), 70–6; V. Branca, *Poliziano e l'umanesimo della parola* (Turin: Einaudi, 1983); E. Donato, 'Death and History in Poliziano's *Stanze*,' *MLN* 80 (1965), 27–40; M. Martelli, *Studi laurenziani* (Florence: Olschki, 1965); O.Z. Pugliese, 'Ambiguità di Bacco nel *Trionfo* laurenziano e nell'arte rinascimentale,' in *Letteratura italiana e arti figurative*, ed. A. Franceschetti (Florence: Olschki, 1988), I, 397–404. Cf. also Karla Langedijk, 'Baccio Bandinelli's Orpheus: A Political Message,' *Mitteilungen des Kunsthistorischen Institutes in Florenz* 20 (1976), 33–52, and Thomas M. Greene, *The Light in Troy* (New Haven and London: Yale University Press, 1982).

1 See D.P. Walker, 'Orpheus the Theologian,' in *The Ancient Theology: Studies in Christian Platonism from the Fifteenth to the Eighteenth Century* (Ithaca, N.Y.: Cornell University Press, 1972), pp. 22–41.

2 On this whole question, see Gary Tomlinson, *Music in Renaissance Magic: Toward a Historiography of Others* (Chicago and London: University of Chicago Press, 1993).

3 Cf. Marsilio Ficino, *Three Books on Life*, ed. and trans. Carol V. Kaske and John R. Clark (Binghamton, NY: Medieval and Renaissance Texts and Studies, 1989), p. 361.

4 Louis E. Lord, *A Translation of the Orpheus of Angelo Politian* (London: Oxford University Press, 1931), p. 86.

5   On the polarization of Plato and Aristotle in Poliziano, see Mario Martelli, *Angelo Poliziano: Storia e metastoria* (Lecce: Conte Editore, 1995).

2 ARIOSTO AND MACHIAVELLI

1   This quotation from *The Prince* and all subsequent quotations are taken from Niccolò Machiavelli, *Il principe e altri scritti*, ed. Gennaro Sasso (Florence: La Nuova Italia, 1965). The translations from Machiavelli are taken from *The Portable Machiavelli*, ed. and trans. Peter Bondanella and Mark Musa (New York: Penguin Books, 1979), pp. 126–7.

2   The Italian passage from *Orlando Furioso* as well as all other subsequent quotations from it are taken from Ludovico Ariosto, *Orlando Furioso*, ed. Cesare Segre (Milan: Mondadori, 1979). The translations are taken from *Orlando Furioso (The Frenzy of Orlando)*, trans. Barbara Reynolds (New York: Penguin Books, 1987).

3   D.S. Carne-Ross, 'The One and the Many: A Reading of *Orlando Furioso*, Cantos 1 and 8,' *Arion* 5, no. 2 (summer 1966), pp. 194–294.

4   The quotations are from *The Stoic Philosophy of Seneca: Essays and Letters of Seneca*, trans. Moses Hadas (Gloucester, Mass.: Peter Smith, 1965), esp. p. 38.

5   The motif of neo-Platonic education in *Orlando Furioso* has been analysed by Albert R. Ascoli, *Ariosto's Bitter Harmony: Crisis and Evasion in the Italian Renaissance* (Princeton: Princeton University Press, 1987).

6   Vincenzo Cartari, *The Fountain of Ancient Fiction*, trans. R. Linche (London, 1599), sig. B-r+v. Cartari restates a worn-out neo-Platonic motif. See, for instance, this formulation from the twelfth-century speculations: 'His (man's) mind and body, though of diverse natures, will be joined into one, such that a mysterious union will render the work harmonious. He shall be both divine and earthly, comprehends the universe about him through knowledge, and commune in worship with the gods ... Brute beasts plainly reveal the grossness of their faculties, their heads cast down, their gaze fixed on the earth; but man alone, his stature bearing witness to the majesty of his mind, will lift up his noble head toward the stars, that he may employ the laws of the spheres and their unalterable courses as a pattern for his own course of life.' *The Cosmographia of Bernardus Silvestris*, trans. Winthrop Wetherbee (New York and London: Columbia University Press, 1973), p. 113.

7   The presence of Erasmus in Ariosto's work has been documented by Pio Rajna, *Le fonti dell'Orlando Furioso*, 2nd ed. (Florence: Sansoni, 1900; repr. 1975, ed.

F. Mazzoni), p. 547. Cf. also the discussion by Giulio Ferroni, 'Ariosto e la concezione umanistica della follia,' in *Atti del Convegno Internazionale 'Ludovico Ariosto'* (Rome: Accademia Nazionale dei Lincei, 1975). In a more general way, cf. Michel Foucault, *Folie et déraison: histoire de la folie à l'âge classique* (Paris: Plon, 1961). Cf. also Jacques Derrida, 'Cogito et histoire de la Folie,' in *L'Écriture et la différence* (Paris: Éditions du Seuil, 1967).

8 Desiderius Erasmus, *The Praise of Folly,* trans. Betty Radice, in *Collected Works of Erasmus,* vol. 27 (Toronto: University of Toronto Press, 1986), p. 149.

9 Among Ariosto scholars that I know of, Peter V. Marinelli is the first to have treated extensively the question of *serio ludere* and laughter in *Orlando Furioso.* See his rich and suggestive study, *Ariosto and Boiardo: The Origins of Orlando Furioso* (Columbia: University of Missouri Press, 1987). For a more general understanding of play, see my *The World at Play: A Study of Boccaccio's Decameron* (Princeton: Princeton University Press, 1986). See also the more systematic formulations by Mihai Spariosu, *Dionysus Reborn: Play and the Esthetic Dimension in Modern Philosophical and Scientific Discourse* (Ithaca and London: Cornell University Press, 1989). Cf. also Roger Caillois, *Man, Play, and Games,* trans. Meyer Barash (New York: Schocken Books, 1979), for a typology of games – *agon, alea, mimicry, ilinx, and simulations.* Caillois misses entirely the aesthetic dimension of play.

10 On Castiglione see Thomas M. Greene, '*Il Cortegiano* and the Choice of a Game,' *Renaissance Quarterly* 32, no. 2 (summer, 1979), 173–86. More generally, see also Wayne Rebhorn, *Courtly Performances: Masking and Festivity in Castiglione's 'Book of the Courtier'* (Detroit: Wayne State University Press, 1978).

11 This episode has been analysed with subtlety by Barbara Pavlock, *Eros, Imitation, and the Epic Tradition* (Ithaca and London: Cornell University Press, 1990), pp. 147–86.

3 ADVENTURES OF UTOPIA

1 This quotation from *The Prince* and all subsequent quotations are taken from Niccolò Machiavelli, *Il principe e altri scritti,* ed. Gennaro Sasso (Florence: La Nuova Italia, 1965). The translations from Machiavelli are taken from *The Portable Machiavelli,* ed. and trans. Peter Bondanella and Mark Musa (New York: Penguin Books, 1979), pp. 126–7.

2 On this issue of the reception of Machiavelli, see Robert Bireley, *The Counter-Reformation Prince: Anti-Machiavellianism on Catholic Statecraft in Early Modern Europe* (Chapel Hill: University of North Carolina Press, 1990). For further bib-

liography, see my *The New Map of the World: The Poetic Philosophy of Giambattista Vico* (Princeton: Princeton University Press, 1999), especially pp. 66–71.

3 Francis Bacon, *The Great Instauration and New Atlantis*, ed. J. Weinberger (Arlington Heights, Ill.: Harlan Davidson, 1980), p. 36. For an excellent discussion of Bacon, see Charles Whitney, *Francis Bacon and Modernity* (New Haven: Yale University Press, 1986). See also Jerry Weinberger, *Science, Fate, and Politics: Francis Bacon and the Utopian Roots of the Modern Age*, a Commentary on Bacon's Advancement of Learning (Ithaca: Cornell University Press, 1985).

4 Tommaso Campanella, *La città del sole: Dialogo poetico / The City of the Sun: A Poetic Dialogue*, trans. with an introduction by Daniel J. Donno (Berkeley, Los Angeles, London: University of California Press, 1981). For a detailed discussion of Campanella's text, see my 'Liminalità e utopia della letteratura,' *Intersezioni* 19, no. 3 (1999), pp. 363–78.

4 THE LUDIC PERSPECTIVE

1 'I am no sorcerer to enjoy travelling through the air. And what will my islemen say where they learn that the governor goes roaming down the winds? And another thing: it is 9000 and odd miles from here to Candaya, and supposing the horse should tire or the giant be in a bad mood, we might be half a dozen years before we got back, and then there would be no isle or islesmen in the world to recognize me.' (II, XLI). Miguel de Cervantes Saavedra, *Don Quixote*, trans. J. M. Cohen (Baltimore, Md.: Penguin Books, 1970), p. 727.

2 I am citing from H.W. Fowler and F.G. Fowler, *The Works of Lucian of Samosata*, vol. 3 (Oxford: Clarendon Press, 1905), pp. 299–301.

3 Leon Battista Alberti, *On Painting*, trans. by John R. Spenser (New Haven and London: Yale University Press, 1956), p. 93. Cf. Alfonso Procaccini, 'Alberti and the "Framing" of Perspective,' *The Journal of Aesthetics and Art Criticism* 30 (1981), 29–39. For an illuminating discussion of *perspectiva*, see Hubert Damisch, *The Origin of 'Perspective,'* trans. John Goodman (Cambridge, Mass.: The MIT Press, 1994).

4 Leo Spitzer, 'Linguistic Perspectivism in *Don Quixote*,' in *Linguistic and Literary History* (Princeton: Princeton University Press, 1948), pp. 41–73.

5 Polydore Vergil. *De rerum inventoribus*, trans. John Langley (New York: Agathynian Club, 1986). See also Denys Hay, *Polydore Vergil: Renaissance Historian and Man of Letters* (Oxford: Clarendon Press, 1985). Above all see Brian P.

Copenhaver, 'The Historiography of Discovery in the Renaissance: The Sources and Composition of Polydore Vergil's *De rerum inventoribus*, I–III,' *Journal of the Warburg and Courtald Institutes* 41 (1978), 192–214.

6 Cervantes, *Don Quixote*, ed. Joseph R. Jones and Kenneth Douglas (New York: Norton, 1981), p. 655. See the reflections on the modern subject by Anthony J. Cascardi in *The Subject of Modernity* (Cambridge: Cambridge University Press, 1992). Cf. also by Cascardi, *The Bounds of Reason: Cervantes, Dostoevsky, Flaubert* (New York: Columbus University Press, 1986).

7 Desiderius Erasmus, *The Education of a Christian Prince*, trans. Neil M. Cheshine and Michael J. Heath, in *Collected Works of Erasmus*, vol. 27, p. 250.

Primary Texts

Alberti, Leon Battista. *On Painting*. Trans. by John R. Spenser. New Haven and London: Yale University Press, 1956.

Ariosto, Ludovico. *Orlando Furioso*. Ed. Cesare Segre. Milan: Mondadori, 1979.

– *The Frenzy of Orlando*. Trans. Barbara Reynolds. New York: Penguin Books, 1987.

Aristotle. *Metaphysics*. Trans. Hugh Tredennick. Loeb Classical Library. Cambridge, Mass.: Harvard University Press, 1935-6.

Bacon, Francis. *The Works of Francis Bacon*. Ed. James Spedding. 7 vols. London: Longman, 1858.

– *The Great Instauration and New Atlantis*. Ed. J. Weinberger. Arlington Heights, Ill.: Harlan Davidson, 1980.

Campanella, Tommaso. *La città del sole: dialogo poetico / The City of the Sun: A Poetic Dialogue*. Trans. with an introduction by Daniel J. Donno. Berkeley, Los Angeles, London: University of California Press, 1981.

Cartari, Vincenzo. *The Fountain of Ancient Fiction*. Trans. R. Linche. London: Adam Islip, 1599.

Cervantes, Miguel de. *El ingenioso hidalgo Don Quixote de la Mancha* . Ed. Martin de Riquer. Barcelona: Clásicos Universales Planeta, 1980.

– *Don Quixote*. Trans. J.M. Cohen. Baltimore, Md.: Penguin Books, 1970.

– *Don Quixote*. Ed. Joseph R. Jones and Kenneth Douglas. New York: Norton, 1981.

Erasmus, Desiderius. *The Education of a Christian Prince* . Trans. Neil M. Cheshire and Michael J. Heath. In *Collected Works of Erasmus*. Vol. 27, ed. A.H.T. Levi. Toronto: University of Toronto Press, 1986.

– *The Praise of Folly*. Trans. Betty Radice. In *Collected Works of Erasmus*. Vol. 27. Toronto: University of Toronto Press, 1986.

Ficino, Marsilio. *Libri de vita triplici*. In *Opera omnia*. Vol. 1. Basel: H. Petri, 1576.

– *Three Books on Life* . Ed. and trans. Carol V. Kaske and John R. Clark. Binghamton, NY: Medieval and Renaissance Texts and Studies, 1989.

– *Platonica theologia de immortalitate.* Florence: Miscomini, 1482.

– *Sopra lo amore o ver Convito di Platone.* Florence: Neri Dortelata, 1544.

– *El libro dell'amore.* 1544. Ed. S. Niccoli. Florence: Olschki, 1987.

– *The Letters.* Vols. 1–6. Trans. Language Dept. of Economic Science. London: Shepheard-Walwyn, 1976.

Galilei, Galileo. *Sidereus Nuncius or The Sidereal Messenger.* Trans. Albert Van Helden. Chicago and London: University of Chicago Press, 1989.

Lorenzo de' Medici. *Selected Poems and Prose.* Ed. and trans. John Thiem. University Park, Pa.: Pennsylvania State University, 1991.

Lucian of Samosata. *The Works of Lucian of Samosata.* Vol. III. Ed. H.W. Fowler and F.G. Fowler. Oxford: Clarendon Press, 1905.

Machiavelli, Niccolò. *Il principe e altri scritti.* Ed. Gennaro Sasso. Florence: La Nuova Italia, 1965.

– *The Prince.* In *The Portable Machiavelli.* Ed. and trans. Peter Bondanella and Mark Musa. New York: Penguin Books, 1979.

Pico della Mirandola, Giovanni. *Opera omnia (De hominis dignitate etc.).* Ed. Eugenio Garin. 2 vols. Turin: Bottega d'Erasmo, 1971.

Plato. *The Collected Dialogues of Plato.* Ed. Edith Hamilton and Huntington Cairns. Bollingen Series 71. 1961. Reprint, Princeton, NJ: Princeton University Press, 1971.

Politian, Angelo. *A Translation of the Orpheus.* London: Oxford University, 1931.

Poliziano, Angelo. *Poesie volgari.* Vol. I. Testi (*Stanze per la giostra; Fabula di Orfeo*). Ed. Francesco Bausi. Manziana (Rome): Vecchiarelli, 1997.

Ribadeneira, Pedro de. *Tratado de la religion y virtudes que debe tener el principe cristiano para gobernar y conservar sus estados, contra lo que Nicolas Maquiavelo y los políticos deste tiempo enseñan.* In *Obras escogidas del Padre Pedro de Rivadeneira,* ed. Don Vicente de la Fuente, pp. 449–587. Madrid, 1868. Reprint, Madrid: Biblioteca de los autores cristianos, 1952.

Seneca, Lucius Annaeus. *Seneca's Tragedies.* Trans. Frank Justus Miller. 2 vols. The Loeb Classical Library. London: Heinemann, 1927.

Shakespeare, William. *The Tempest.* Signet Classic. Ed. R. Langbaum. New York: The New American Library, 1964.

Vergil, Polydore. *De rerum inventoribus.* Trans. John Langley. New York: Agathynian Club, 1986.

www.ingramcontent.com/pod-product-compliance
Ingram Content Group UK Ltd.
Pitfield, Milton Keynes, MK11 3LW, UK
UKHW031842110225
454967UK00001B/49